CONTENTS

Introduction 4

1 **History** 5
Indians and Slaves 5
Independence 9
Getúlio Vargas 14
Military Dictatorship 17

2 **Society** 20
Indians 20
Women 23
Children 25
Race 27
Religion 28

3 **Politics** 37
Two Brazils 37
The Return to Democracy 39
Grassroots Movements 41

4 **The Economy** 45
Boom and Bust 45
Industrialization 47
Inequality 51

5 **Amazon and Environment** 53
Myths and Legends 53
Concrete Jungles 59

6 **Culture** 61
Carnival 61
Literature 63
Football (soccer) 66
Gambling 68
Food and Drink 70

Brazil in 2000 71
Where to Go, What to See 75
Tips for Travelers 78
Addresses and Contacts 80
Further Reading and Bookstores 81
Facts and Figures 82

INTRODUCTION

"Next stop, Paradise", barks a matter-of-fact voice over the intercom of the train on the São Paulo Underground. Nowadays Paradise is just a rather dingy district of downtown São Paulo, a station on the North-South Metro line, but when the first explorers reached Brazil five hundred years ago, they thought it was the real thing. They found friendly, beautiful natives, an abundance of fruit and fertile soil. Travelers ever since have marveled at the beauty of Rio de Janeiro, gazed in awe at the vastness of the Amazon river and delighted in the palm-fringed beaches of the Northeast.

Few other countries are as close to being an earthly paradise, yet for millions of Brazilians life in the land of plenty means a struggle for survival. One of the six largest countries in the world, Brazil is blessed with millions of acres of fertile land, hundreds of rushing rivers, minerals of every sort, and is free of natural disasters like earthquakes or hurricanes. Yet millions live in overcrowded fetid slums, squeezed into the unwanted spaces of the big cities – under bridges, clinging to steep hillsides, on the banks of sewage-choked streams, next to rubbish dumps, or in daily fear of floods and mud-slides.

The gap between rich and poor is the widest on earth, with the wealthiest one per cent earning more than the poorest fifty per cent. Brazil is a land of baffling paradoxes. It is free of the religious, racial, or ethnic divisions that have brought civil war to other countries, yet violence is the major cause of death among young males. In the last twenty years, over a thousand trade unionists, religious workers, rights activists, and indigenous leaders have been assassinated for political reasons. It is a major world food producer, but millions of its own people go hungry. It covers an area of 3.3 million square miles, yet two-thirds of the population of 156 million live in towns and cities. It has the tenth largest economy but social indicators comparable with some of the poorest countries in the world. Economically dynamic, socially Brazil stagnates.

The explanation for these riddles lies in Brazil's history. Slavery lasted longer and was more widespread than in any other country of the Western Hemisphere. It was only abolished just over 100 years ago. The attitudes that went with slavery grew so deeply entrenched that they still influence the mentality of today's Brazilians. Brazil never had a political or cultural revolution, or any violent rupture of the status quo. Slavery was abolished, but what took its place was not equality and fraternity, but an unofficial system of first- and second-class citizenship, a social apartheid more difficult to fight than any official system of discrimination. Parts of Brazil are as modern as anywhere in the industrialized world, but life for many Brazilians is still rooted in the past.

1 HISTORY

Exploring the unknown world in their cramped craft, the Portuguese navigators were the astronauts of the fifteenth century. At Sagres, a medieval NASA built on the westernmost tip of Portugal, they perfected new navigation instruments, developed modern map-making, and calculated the circumference of the world, when officially it was still flat. In the medieval spice race, Portugal and Spain competed to find new, faster routes to the Indies, pushing back the frontiers of the known world. The monotonous European diet craved spices – pepper, nutmeg, cloves, and cinnamon – not only for their flavor, but because they were invaluable for preserving meat during the winter. Tea, sugar, chocolate, potatoes, and coffee were still unknown.

In 1500 a fleet of Portuguese ships on its way to the East round the Cape of Good Hope, commanded by Pedro Alvares Cabral, was blown off course and sighted land: by accident, Europe had "discovered" Brazil. Baptized the "Land of the True Cross" (Terra da Vera Cruz), the new land at first seemed disappointing: no gold or silver in sight, just lots of friendly natives, fruit, and forests. The only commercially viable product was a reddish wood. Because of its color they called it cinderwood, *pau brasa*, and so the new land became Brasil (in Portuguese), or Brazil (in English). A few trading posts were set up, but it was an inauspicious beginning to a country which would eventually supply the gold to finance Britain's Industrial Revolution, the rubber that made possible the motorcar, and which would feed the world with sugar and coffee. Brazilwood quickly gave way to sugar. Sugar plantations needed labor but the Indians who had welcomed the white man to their land were hunters and gatherers and resisted recruitment. Peaceful co-existence was over.

Indians and Slaves

Slaving expeditions were organized, and the hunters became the hunted. Nobody really knows how many million Indians there were when the Europeans arrived, but today there are just over 300,000 left. The Catholic missionaries who had come with the Portuguese explorers and settlers had a problem. Could the Indians be enslaved if they had souls? Did they have souls if they worshiped pagan gods and lived as primitives? The Jesuits decided that Indians did have souls and set about converting them, gathering thousands of Guarani Indians into fortified settlements known as "reductions." The Indians worked the land, became literate, studied music and learnt crafts. But the plantation owners needed slaves, not musicians, and the reductions were regularly raided and destroyed.

By claiming that Indians had souls, the Jesuits became an embarrassment, standing in the way of development. Accused of setting up a state within the state, in 1759 they were expelled from Brazil by the Portuguese Crown, as they had been from the Spanish-speaking colonies. Priests in chains were shipped back to Europe and the first of Latin America's many attempts at building Utopia ended in flames. The slavers became Brazil's first explorers, sailing thousands of miles upriver in search of Indians and gold. They became known as *bandeirantes,* because they carried the flags (*bandeiras*) of their patrons on their expeditions. They were a bloodthirsty lot, killing and enslaving wherever they went – one boasted of possessing 30,000 dried human ears. Nevertheless, the word "bandeirante" has heroic associations today, especially in São Paulo, whose early development was based on their activities.

By the seventeenth century, Brazil was Europe's leading sugar supplier and Portugal's most important colony. To meet the need for labor, slave ships brought Africans in ever increasing numbers. One historian calculates that forty per cent of the estimated 9,500,000 slaves transported to the New World went to Brazil. Others believe that up to 13 million men, women, and children were imported during slavery's 350-year reign in Brazil, before abolition in 1888. They were counted not as individuals, but as merchandise, by weight, and referred to as "*peças,*" pieces. Many years later the Nazis also referred to their Jewish prisoners loaded into cattle wagons for transport to the death camps as *stucken*, pieces.

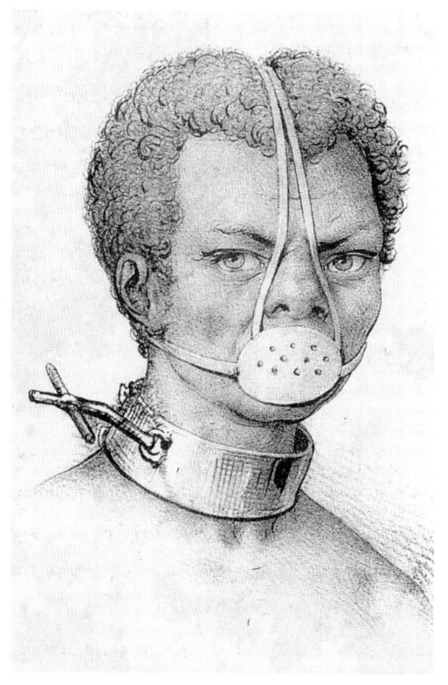

Punishment of a slave

Brazil imported six times more Africans than the United States, double the number that went to the Spanish colonies or the British West Indies. Originally intended for the sugar plantations, they ended up wherever there was economic activity. For four centuries, Brazil's immense wealth was accumulated by the work of slaves. They cut cane, panned for gold, and picked cotton and coffee. They were porters for the bandeirantes and tilled fields for priests and monks. In the towns, they worked as cooks, house servants, nursemaids, street sellers, sedan chair carriers, water carriers, and laborers. Slaves were the hands and the feet of their masters. With Indians, they made up the bulk of the army in Brazil's war against Paraguay in 1865.

On arrival from Africa, people from the same tribe were separated to make rebellion difficult. They spoke different languages, they came from

Slaves on a coffee-plantation

different regions, they had different customs, but they were united by their suffering and in their revolt at the inhuman conditions to which they were subjected. The average life span of a plantation slave was between seven and eight years. Many came with trades: they were artisans, goldsmiths, silversmiths, blacksmiths. In the gold region of Minas Gerais, they built the baroque churches that still stand today. "The Brazilian dream was to have one or two slaves whose labor could be hired out for a price high enough to free the dreamer from ever having to work. Begging was preferable to work. Even beggars had slaves," wrote Pedro I, Brazil's first post-independence ruler.

Clovis Moura, a black sociologist, believes that slavery became the blueprint for Brazilian society. It provided the dominant ethos, laid the foundations for economic inequality and exploitation, and influenced the way institutions, groups, and classes developed after abolition.

Slave Rebellion

Generations of Brazilian schoolchildren studied history books that omitted a whole side of slavery – the many revolts, rebellions and uprisings and the existence of the *quilombos*. Free territories set up by groups of runaway slaves, the quilombos took root all over Brazil. Their direct descendants can still be found in remote villages today, using the odd word of Bantu or Nagô. The runaways defended themselves from attacks and raided plantations, stealing food and killing the owners.

Zumbi and Palmares

The most famous and longest surviving quilombo was the Republic of Palmares, which lasted from 1630-1695, with up to 30,000 people in dozens of villages scattered over an area of 17,000 square miles in what is now the state of Alagoas. Even Indians and poor whites came to join the runaway slaves. Plantations and villages were raided for women, but the sexual imbalance was so great that polyandry became the custom, each woman having up to five husbands. Palmares developed its own language, a mixture of Bantu and Portuguese. The ex-slaves fed themselves by hunting, fishing, and farming, made pottery and baskets, wove clothes and forged iron. They made musical instruments and weapons with which to defend themselves. For a few years, solidarity, equality, and cooperation replaced the degradation and exploitation of the plantations.

But for Brazil's rulers, Palmares was diabolical and dangerous, a permanent incentive to revolt which had to be destroyed and its memory erased. Supported by the Church and the plantation owners, they organized armies of bandeirantes, mercenaries, and criminals to do the job. In 1695, after several expeditions, Palmares was finally overrun. All the inhabitants were killed or enslaved, and the severed head of Zumbi, its legendary leader, was put on display to terrorize black Brazilians, who had come to believe that he was immortal.

In a way he was. Three hundred years later, Zumbi is officially a national hero and Brazil's rulers make pilgrimages to the site of Palmares. Even after the most famous quilombo was destroyed, slaves continued to escape. In 1741 the King of Portugal ordered all runaways to be branded with the letter F for *Fujão* (runaway). Nineteenth century newspapers carried columns of "wanted" advertisements for runaway slaves which convey an idea of the treatment they were fleeing from. The *Diário de Pernambuco* of May 23, 1839 offered a reward for a runaway called Joana, who had "burn marks on her breasts and few front teeth." In 1870 the same paper was looking for a slave called Germano, aged 17 or 18, "with a sad look, big feet, long legs and marks of recent punishment on his buttocks."

Abolition

In 1850 the British banned the international slave trade and blockaded Brazilian ports, but slaves continued to be smuggled in. Inside Brazil, the abolition campaign was gathering momentum, but slaves were not finally freed until 1888. By then only five per cent of the 14 million Brazilians were slaves, down from a third in 1850, due to European immigration and the release of slaves prior to abolition.

Slave owners had predicted disaster when the traffic ended, but instead the end of investment in human suffering freed capital for investment in infrastructure and encouraged the immigration of free workers. While slaves had been captive, land was free to anyone who occupied it; once they were free, land had to be paid for. After abolition, some slaves were kept on by their former masters as employees, but many were abandoned, without money, jobs, land, or homes. A new vagrancy law was enacted, making anyone without a fixed address and work liable to arrest. The law is still on the statute books.

Independence

One of the reasons slavery lasted longer in Brazil than anywhere else in the Americas was the survival of the monarchy. Long after all the other colonies of Latin America had become republics, Brazil was ruled by an Emperor. The American War of Independence and the French Revolution had been over for a century when Brazil finally became a republic in 1889. The delay was not for want of trying. Like the Americans, Brazilians objected to the taxes imposed by Lisbon and resented the ban on any industry or indeed learning in Portugal's richest colony. Printing presses, bookstores, universities, and foreign newspapers were all forbidden.

Tiradentes

In 1792 the small town of Vila Rica, now known as Ouro Preto, was the center of Brazil's lucrative gold industry. There, a group of prominent citizens, including lawyers, a priest, and landowners, began plotting for independence. They rejected Portuguese taxes and demanded the right to build factories, universities, and steel mills. The rebels even sent emissaries to ask the newly independent USA's Thomas Jefferson for military aid in exchange for future trade preferences.

The conspiracy foundered when they were betrayed and arrested, and the Crown decided to make an example of one of them. A young military officer called Joaquim José da Silva Xavier, better known as Tiradentes, the Toothpuller, was hung, drawn, and quartered and his descendants officially cursed (only recently was the curse withdrawn). While his fellow conspirators are forgotten, Tiradentes is now Brazil's national hero. He was also the only one of the rebel band who thought that independence should also mean an end to slavery. Six years after his death, inspired by the successful slave rebellion in Haiti as well as the French Revolution, slaves in Salvador staged an uprising which failed. After that, none of the many rebellions against the Portuguese and the Brazilian monarchy ever seriously threatened royal rule.

Dom Pedro I, the first emperor of independent Brazil

Courtesy of South American Pictures

Royal Independence

Instead it fell to Napoleon to consolidate Brazil's unique variety of royal independence. To escape from his triumphant advance through the Iberian Peninsula in 1808, the entire Royal Portuguese Court of 15,000 people fled to Brazil aboard a fleet of ships, led by King João VI. Suddenly Brazil was no longer a distant colony, but the center of the Portuguese empire. All around Brazil, the Spanish colonies were fighting for independence, but the presence of the monarchy gave Brazil metropolitan status, allowing it to trade directly with other countries.

When the Napoleonic Wars were over and the King returned to Lisbon in 1821, the Portuguese tried unsuccessfully to turn the clock back and return their richest possession to colonial status. Left behind as regent, the King's son, Pedro, soon realized that his best move was to lead the burgeoning movement for independence, rather than oppose it. Instead of the bloody warfare that ravaged the other Latin American countries, Brazil, so the story goes, became independent in 1822 with a single shout – the *Grito do Ipiranga*, the river where Pedro allegedly yelled his melodramatic "Independence or Death."

The monarchy lasted another 67 years. Acting as a focus for loyalty and political unity, it prevented the vast country, which shared borders with ten other colonies, ex-colonies, and independent states, from breaking up. It also enabled an aristocratic white class to prolong its rule over a slave society. Brazil was free from Portugal, but most Brazilians had yet to become free citizens. Pedro I's son, Pedro II, did not see why slavery should be abolished, even though he championed the latest technological inventions. Under his rule, Brazil became the second country after England to introduce postage stamps. The Emperor was the first Brazilian to have a telephone installed, and encouraged the spread of the railways. Brazil was modernizing, but slavery continued.

The Republic

By the 1880s, coffee had long surpassed sugar and gold as Brazil's most important product, and the São Paulo coffee planters had become the most powerful political and economic group in the country. They wanted a republic, and once slavery was gone, pressure grew to abolish another anachronism (the monarchy). The Republican movement found allies among military officers who had served in the war against Paraguay and were discontent with government policy. On November 15, 1889 "in the name of the people, the army, and the navy," Emperor Pedro II was deposed and given 24 hours to leave the country, and a provisional republic, headed by Marshal Deodoro da Fonseca, a war hero, was installed. Church and state were separated and the Republic of Brazil was formally created in February 1891 with a constitution drawn up by a Constituent Assembly. With the monarchy went the Catholic Church's status as the official religion. The republicans turned instead to positivism, preferring scientific rationalism to religious belief. The country's new flag, with its motto "Order and Progress," was inspired by the new thinking.

Antônio the Counselor

The monarchy had gone, southern cities now had gas lighting, telephones, and electric trams, but in the Northeast, the home of Brazil's first cycle of sugar wealth, little had changed. Landowners were authoritarian patriarchs, some of them despots, and most of the population lived in extreme poverty, worsened by a devastating drought in 1877. Thousands emigrated to the Amazon, where the rubber boom was in full swing, or to the south. Those who stayed, starved.

Without help from the government, the landowners, or the Church, people turned to mysticism. They began to follow a man with a flowing beard and rough robes who roamed the *sertão* (drylands) preaching that the end of the world would come in the year 1900. Hundreds, then thousands, flocked to hear the charismatic Antônio Maciel, who became known as the *Conselheiro* (Counselor). What began as a religious movement developed into a challenge to the existing social and political system of the Northeast.

The Conselheiro talked about the need for a better life in the here and now. He protested by tearing down the public notices announcing tax increases. The Church declared him a subversive, while the state governor wanted him locked up in a mental asylum. As thousands abandoned their homes to follow the preacher, landowners feared a labor shortage. In 1893 the band was attacked by soldiers and the Counselor realized he must find a sanctuary. Like an Old Testament prophet, he led his followers on a five-week march into the sertão until they came to an isolated valley surrounded by five mountain ranges. Within two years, the city of Canudos founded by the Counselor and his followers had become one of the largest towns in Bahia, boasting 20,000 inhabitants, two churches, and a thriving economy which even exported goatskins to Europe.

Visitors reported in wonder, "there are neither rich or poor, the land belongs to all, there is no hunger or misery, no money, no police or thieves, no locks on doors, no brothels, no alcohol, everyone is happy in a big brotherhood." A five-hour working day left time for prayers and leisure. There were schools for the children. The Counselor had modeled Canudos on Thomas More's *Utopia*, which he had read.

But there was no place for Utopia in the Brazilian Northeast. By offering the example of a successful but egalitarian society, Canudos threatened the existing system of exploitation, hunger, ignorance, and wealth for the few. Like Palmares before it, Canudos had to be destroyed, before the example could spread. In Rio de Janeiro, the capital, Canudos was used as an excuse by the military to attack the remaining monarchists. The Counselor and his followers were portrayed as a bunch of dangerous fanatics, plotting to overthrow the republic and restore the monarchy, helped by foreign military advisers.

Yet the apparently easy task of wiping out a backlands rebellion turned instead into the Brazilian army's biggest and bloodiest campaign since the war against Paraguay, twenty years earlier. The men and women of Canudos resisted with improvised guerrilla tactics and rustic weapons, harassing the soldiers as they approached the town through the canyons and hills. It took four military expeditions over a year to overrun Utopia, costing the lives of nearly ten thousand men.

The End of Canudos

The final, victorious expedition in 1897 brought together ten thousand soldiers drawn from eleven different states, and 19 heavy cannon. As they advanced through the dry inhospitable *sertão*, they passed the skeletons of soldiers from the previous expeditions. Twelve days before the final attack, the Counselor died. Once the government troops had taken the city, after fierce hand-to-hand fighting, they set fire to it, killed most of the survivors, and handed out the children as booty. Many ended up as prostitutes. For the Counselor's followers, the end of the world had come three years early. The Counselor's body was disinterred and his head cut off and examined unsuccessfully for signs of madness.

The battle for Canudos was reported in Europe, where *The Times* of London named him "the Backlands Messiah," and criticized the manipulation of the uprising to attack monarchists. Official Brazilian history labeled

Canudos a story of religious fanaticism, and in his book *Os Sertões,* which became a classic, journalist Euclides da Cunha attributed the movement to madness brought on by racial mixing. A twelve mile-long dam now covers the ruins of the town. Beside it is a new town, Nova Canudos, which exhibits the same misery, backwardness, and ignorance that led to the founding of Canudos a hundred years ago. Today the Northeast still has the worst inequality, illiteracy, and hunger in Brazil.

The Rubber Boom

Thousands of miles west of Canudos, the need for rubber to make pneumatic tires for Europe and America's newly invented motorcars was making fortunes in the Amazon rainforest. English and American companies set up trading posts along the rivers, enlisting Indians to collect the rubber in a system of virtual slavery. The Amazon capital Manaus, a small settlement on the edge of the river, flourished. Solid European-style buildings and an extravagantly beautiful opera house appeared among the huts and boats. Famous opera stars traveled across the Atlantic and a thousand miles upriver to sing there. The sidewalk around the opera house was paved with rubber tiles to muffle the sound of the horses' hooves as the carriages drew up. The rich sent their laundry to Paris, while ships brought back German sausages, hats from Paris, and Polish prostitutes.

The boom lasted until 1912, when cheaper rubber grown from thousands of saplings smuggled out of the Amazon to Kew Gardens by an Englishman called Wickham Steed began to inundate the market. Malaya, where the saplings had flourished, soon dominated the world market and Manaus sank back into torpor. Millions of dollars had been earned by the rubber barons at the cost of thousands of Indian lives, but little had changed.

Traditional rubber processing in the Amazon *Mary Evans Picture Library*

Supplying rubber for the West's vehicles was not Brazil's only contribution to advancing technology. Competing with the Wright brothers, Alberto Santos Dumont made the first registered flight in a heavier-than-air machine in Paris in 1906. He also invented the wristwatch to keep his hands free for flying. Years later he committed suicide, grieved by the use of his invention for making war.

European Immigration

Exports of coffee and other agricultural products still dominated the Brazilian economy in the first few decades of the twentieth century, but coffee wealth had stimulated industry and thousands of factories were opening, attracting a flood of immigrants. Between 1888, when slaves were freed, and 1928, 3.5 million people arrived in Brazil, principally Italians, Portuguese, Spanish, Germans, and Japanese. The new expanding urban classes had more in common with their counterparts in Europe and North America than with the landowners and the dirt-poor peasantry of the countryside. Italian and Spanish anarchists soon dominated the factories and led the first strikes for better conditions, but failed to threaten the rural elites who still controlled political power.

The Prestes Column

After overthrowing the monarchy, the military was impatient for change. In 1924 an army officer named Luis Carlos Prestes led a rebellion against the federal government, demanding social and economic reforms. The rebels marched through the backlands of Brazil, attacking and occupying towns, traveling over 15,000 miles in three years. The 1500 men who began the march were devastated by cholera and eventually sought exile in Bolivia. Prestes later became Secretary General of the Brazilian Communist Party (PCB), after spending three years in Moscow. In the 1930s he was imprisoned for nine years while his wife, Olga Benário, a German Jew, was deported back to die in Ravensbruck concentration camp.

Getúlio Vargas

The unbroken rule of the rural oligarchies of São Paulo and Minas Gerais, known as the coffee-with-milk alliance because of their respective products, was finally overthrown by a man from the southern state of Rio Grande do Sul in 1930. When Getúlio Vargas' troops tethered their horses to the monuments of São Paulo and Rio, they opened a new chapter in Brazilian history.

[illegible]rmer deputy, minister, and governor, in Rio Grande do Sul, Vargas [illegible]or fifteen years, first as constitutional president, then as dictator, fol-[illegible] a failed Communist uprising by military officers in 1937. His "New [illegible] inspired by Italian Fascism, lasted until the end of the Second World [illegible]argas reorganized the trade unions along corporatist lines, run by men hand-picked to collaborate with the government. Strikes were banned but working conditions were improved, and labor rights introduced, including the minimum wage.

The Fascist influence of the time is still visible in Brazil, not only in the structure of the trade unions, but in some of its public buildings. In the Governor's Palace in João Pessoa, capital of Paraíba state, the ornamental tiled floor incorporates a swastika design.

Getúlio Vargas AP

The Second World War

After 1937 Vargas stamped out opposition, closed Congress, and political prisoners were routinely tortured by his dreaded head of secret police, Filinto Muller. For the first three years of the Second World War Brazil maintained relations with the Axis powers, but in 1942 U.S. economic pressure forced Vargas to allow Allied air bases on the northeast coast, the nearest point to Africa. In retaliation, German submarines attacked Brazilian merchant ships off the coast, killing over 600 people. Brazil declared war on Germany and sent a contingent of 25,000 men to fight with the Allies in the invasion of Italy in 1944, the only Latin American country to do so.

In the Amazon, 30,000 tappers recruited in the Northeast temporarily revived the dying rubber industry to supply the Allies, cut off from their Asian plantations by the Japanese invasion of Malaya. Dumped in the rainforest, thousands of the northeasterners died from malaria, attacks by wild animals, and hunger. In exchange for Brazilian collaboration and raw materials, the U.S. financed the infant steel industry and by the 1950s industry had overtaken agriculture in economic importance.

Vargas invested in infrastructure and accelerated Brazil's industrialization by establishing powerful state companies. Brazil soon ceased to be a predominantly rural country, as a massive migration began from the countryside to the cities. By the 1980s, three-quarters of the population was living in urban areas.

The post-war clamor for democracy reached Brazil and Vargas had to resign, only to return as elected president in 1950. In his second term in office, Vargas continued to invest in infrastructure and industrialization and widened workers" benefits. In response to nationalist demands, he created the state oil company Petrobras, earning the hostility of the conservative establishment and the Americans. Under political and economic pressure and facing a hostile press and Congress, Vargas, once the all-powerful dictator, felt isolated.

Putting Brazil on the Map

In 1954 he committed suicide, setting off a turbulent period of forty years during which only one elected president, Juscelino Kubitschek, elected to succeed Vargas in 1955, completed his term of office. Kubitschek, whose slogan was "fifty years in five," was an optimistic expansionist who believed in Brazil's destiny as a great country. In three years he built Brasília, a brand new capital set down in the flat empty plains of central Brazil, 700 miles inland from Rio and São Paulo. To finish it on time, bricks were flown in by the plane-load. Construction workers flocked to build Brasília from all over the country and stayed on to become the first inhabitants of the city, living in dormitory suburbs well out of sight of the impressive planned center.

Kubitschek also built the first road link to the Amazon, running from Brasília to Belém, and encouraged the multinational car industry to open factories in São Paulo. He put Brazil on the world map, at the cost of accelerating inflation. Kubitschek was succeeded in 1961 by Jânio Quadros, a charismatic but eccentric populist who mixed campaigns against bikinis and horse racing with a non-aligned foreign policy, decorating Che Guevara, then Cuban Minister of Industry, and supporting Fidel Castro when the U.S. launched the Bay of Pigs invasion in the same year.

Goulart Government

By now inflation was accelerating fast and, accused of planning a coup d'état against a hostile Congress, Quadros surprised everyone by resigning after only eight months in power, blaming "hidden forces" for his downfall. Conservative military officers tried to stop vice-president João Goulart, regarded as a leftist, from taking office, but Goulart's brother-in-law, Leonel Brizola, governor of the state of Rio Grande do Sul, led pressure for the constitution to be respected.

During Goulart's three-year government, Brazil became increasingly polarized between those who wanted radical reforms and those who wanted to uphold the status quo, rejecting reforms as communist-inspired. The Catholic Church was alarmed by what it perceived as the communist threat in the Northeast, where peasant leagues were demanding land reform. Washington shared its suspicions.

Role of the United States

The U.S. government had always reserved for itself the right to determine economic and political policy in its "backyard," Latin America, using a mixture of carrot and stick. After 1945 American policies in the hemisphere were dominated by the Cold War, and above all, after the Cuban Revolution of 1959, by the need to prevent "another Cuba." In 1961 President Kennedy launched the Alliance for Progress, an aid and development program designed to bind Latin American countries into an anti-communist chorus. Peace Corps volunteers were poured into Latin America – Brazil alone received over 600.

The U.S. also tried to stop the threatened nationalization of foreign companies, using a combination of open economic pressure (cutting credits and refusing to renegotiate foreign debt) and covert methods, such as financing local right-wing organizations. Washington wanted Brazil's agricultural policy to provide a market for U.S. farm equipment and U.S. exports like wheat and dairy products. Secretary of State John Foster Dulles is alleged to have once said, "Brazilian desires are secondary, though it is useful to pat them a bit and make them think that you are fond of them." When U.S. interests were threatened by a left-wing government and peasants began calling for land reform, the U.S. backed a military coup.

Military Dictatorship

The coup eventually came in 1964, when the army high command, supported by the conservative classes and backed by the U.S., overthrew Goulart. Once the generals were in command of the economy, they promoted the development of Brazilian industry behind high protectionist barriers, creating the so-called "tripod" of state, national and multinational companies which became the basis for Brazil's much-vaunted "economic miracle." To help the miracle along, unions were stifled, strikes banned, and wages reduced, while censorship banned any but favorable economic news.

For the U.S., Brazil under military rule became an important regional leader and ally in the Cold War. Relations later turned sour when President Jimmy Carter made human rights an issue, and Brazil began to seek a more independent trade policy, looking not only to Europe and Japan, but to the Third World for markets.

The avowed aim of what the generals christened the "Glorious Revolution" was to "restore democracy, reduce inflation, and end corruption." Instead, the long-lasting military regime shattered democratic organizations, fed corruption by introducing press censorship, and left behind, 21 years later, a huge, unpayable foreign debt. Unlike other military dictators, such as Chile's General Pinochet, or Paraguay's Alfredo Stroessner, the Brazilian generals stuck to four-year terms of office, succeeding each other in power.

During the dictatorship, over 20,000 Brazilians were imprisoned, most of them tortured, some were killed, and at least 150 prisoners "disappeared."

Military ceremony during the inauguration of a civilian president in 1985, ending twenty years of military rule *Julio Etchart/Reportage*

Thousands more went into exile, including the current president, Fernando Henrique Cardoso, and several of his ministers.

Urban guerrilla groups appeared after Congress, unions, and every available democratic forum had been closed down by repression and censorship. After making an initial impact by hijacking planes, raiding banks, and kidnapping the American, German, and Swiss ambassadors and exchanging them for political prisoners, the groups were implacably hunted down and eliminated. When eighty guerrillas moved from the cities to the Araguaia region of the Amazon basin in 1972 to begin a Maoist-inspired revolution deep in the forest, they were soon discovered. Fifteen thousand soldiers were deployed in the region, peasant farmers were intimidated and tortured for information, and all the group was killed or captured.

Economic Miracle

Politically pacified, Brazil became the darling of foreign investors because of its "economic miracle," averaging over ten per cent growth rates every year between 1968 and 1973. The middle classes, beneficiaries of growing income inequality, had never had it so good, while the U.S. recognized Brazil as an emerging world power. "Where Brazil goes, there goes the rest of the hemisphere," President Nixon told one of the general-presidents,

Emilio Medici, in 1973. Between 1973 and 1980, Chile, Uruguay, Argentina, and Bolivia all suffered bloody military coups.

Brazil's military had a clear geopolitical plan to turn it into a world power, dominating Latin America and controlling the South Atlantic. The generals also intended to make Brazil a nuclear power, concluding a $10 billion nuclear cooperation agreement with West Germany in preference to signing the Nuclear Non-Proliferation Treaty.

The military planned massive relocations of the population to secure "empty" areas and to ease pressure for land reform. Displaced by dam-building and mechanization for export crops in the south and drought in the Northeast, hundreds of thousands of peasant farmers were encouraged to occupy the Amazon region or cross the border into the fertile lands of Paraguay. Armies of migrant laborers hired to build dams in the Amazon were subsequently left to become itinerant gold prospectors, polluting the rivers and invading Indian reserves.

By the time the military handed power back to a civilian government in 1985, the economy had grown to rank tenth in the world, but wages, health, and education levels had failed to keep up. The military regime left behind a more unequal, more corrupt society with weakened political institutions. A decade-long "safe, gradual" transition from military to civilian rule averted political upheaval or the trial of military personnel for human rights violations. Instead, many of the civilians who had served the regime without opposing its use of torture and repression remained in power.

2 SOCIETY

One hundred years after the end of slavery, Brazilian society is multiracial and complex, but remains hugely unequal. While some young Brazilians are at ease with cellphones and the Internet, others are being shot dead because they want land reform or because they live on the city streets. Most of the population live in towns and cities, but small groups of isolated Indians still wander in the Amazon rainforest.

Indians

Place names like Guanabara, Curitiba, and Cuiabá are a perpetual reminder of Brazil's original inhabitants. Brazilians with not a drop of indigenous blood boast Indian names like Iracema and Moacyr. Manioc flour and the guaraná drink are part of the national diet, and most fish, fruit, and fauna are known by their Indian names. Most people in the North and Northeast still sleep more comfortably in a hammock than a bed.

The Indians now number little more than 300,000, only 0.2 per cent of the total Brazilian population, divided into 200 different groups speaking 170 languages. Relations between the surviving indigenous groups and white society have fluctuated. During nationalist periods they have been romanticized as the most genuine of all Brazilians. In the nineteenth century this produced Brazil's only famous opera, *O Guarani,* by Carlos Gomes, and *Iracema*, a novel by José de Alencar that became a classic. More recently it led to a short-lived attempt to substitute Santa Claus with a home-grown alternative, "Papai Indio."

But in recent years the tide has turned against the Indians. Once the military regime began the drive to conquer the Amazon in the 1970s, Indian communities again came to be seen as obstacles to progress, development, and wealth. Roads were deliberately driven through reserves, spreading disease and introducing alcohol and prostitution. In 1974 the Indians began to fight back. Despite speaking different languages and coming from villages all over Brazil, they found they had something in common: the need to stop their land being invaded by whites.

Land Conflicts

Demarcation was the answer. If indigenous areas were clearly marked out and their boundaries officially recognized, then it would be easier to defend them. But the process has been slow and invasions have continued. In the Greater Amazon region, the Xavantes lost their land to the Italian company

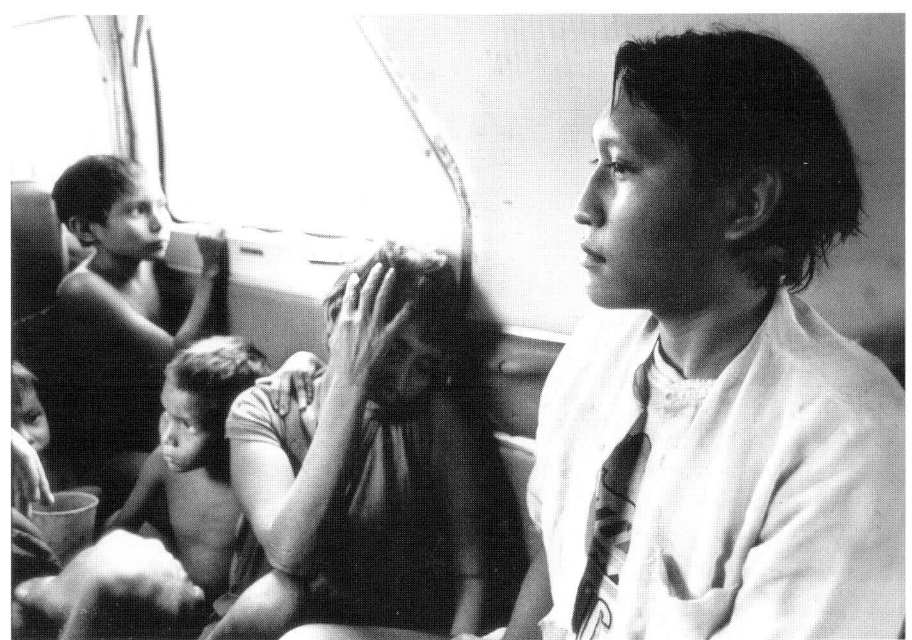

Yanomami Indian family with malaria, being flown to a mission hospital. The disease was introduced by gold prospectors, who invaded their lands

Julio Etchart/ Reportage

Liquigas; the Waimiri Atroari saw part of their reserve flooded by the Balbina dam and now a road is being driven through it by the army, and the Parakanâ were first moved to make way for the Transamazon Highway and then for the Tucuruí dam. The Nambiquara were displaced by ranches and then by the Cuiabá to Santarém highway, the uru-Weu-Wau-Wau and the Zorro were in the way of the World Bank-funded Polonoroeste road and development project.

Invasion and land feuds have brought violence in their wake. In 1988, fourteen Ticuna were murdered by loggers; in 1993, sixteen Yanomami were shot dead by gold prospectors. Individual Indian leaders and several missionaries who worked with Indians have been murdered.

Yanomami

Most of Brazil's indigenous groups have had contact with surrounding society, sometimes over centuries, but there are still small groups of "isolated Indians," glimpsed in remote corners of the Amazon rainforest. In the Northern Amazon live the Yanomami, numbering about 9,000, the last large group of relatively isolated Indians in the Americas. Another 12,000 live over the border in Venezuela. In their communal huts deep in the forest, most Yanomami still live a nomadic, stone age existence, but in 1990 thousands of *garimpeiros* (wildcat gold prospectors), supplied and supported by local businessmen and politicians, began invading their gold-rich territory.

Periodically, when international pressure from environmentalists and development agencies becomes intense, the federal government intervenes to expel the gold miners, but they always return, with devastating results. Over the years at least 1500 Yanomami have succumbed to malaria, TB, influenza, and other diseases to which they have no resistance. Some have been shot dead during clashes. Unable to find fish and game because of the noise and pollution of the rivers, many Yanomami have also died from malnutrition.

Government Policy

In 1996 a change in Indian land rights legislation permitted any person, company, or local authority to lay claim to part of a reserve, if they could come up with documents proving it was theirs. A government memo admitted that the aim was to open the way for economic development "in the areas where most indigenous peoples live" – the Amazon basin.

The change was condemned by everyone from the European Parliament to the Indians themselves, who said it would endanger their lives. An eloquent example of what happens to tribes crowded into smaller and smaller reserves and forced to work in hostile surroundings comes from the Kaiowa Indians in Mato Grosso do Sul. Over the last five years, 250 have committed suicide, most of them teenagers who worked in the local sugar-cane alcohol distilleries.

The National Indian Foundation, FUNAI, the government agency responsible for Brazil's Indians, has a checkered history. Many FUNAI workers have been brave, dedicated people, some giving their lives to protect the Indians. But the agency has become associated with corruption, inefficiency, and a chronic lack of funds. Set up as a guardian of Indian interests, FUNAI officials have all too often conspired against them, in return for bribes from the loggers, ranchers, and garimpeiros. Some Indian groups, too, have allowed loggers and garimpeiros onto their reserves in exchange for pitiable rewards of food, vehicles, or money.

Brazilian law, based on the positivist idea that one nation corresponds to one territory ruled by a single, monolithic state, does not accept the idea of a pluri-ethnic or multi-nation state. Successive governments have tried to integrate Indians into Brazilian society as individuals, effectively denying them any right to communal land or reserves.

The Indians are fighting for their right to be different with growing sophistication. Their organizations, both national and regional, hold regular assemblies, organize protests and demonstrations, and increasingly collabo-

Luiza Erundina, former mayor of São Paulo

Julio Etchart/ Reportage

rate with other popular movements like the *sem terra* (landless peasants) who fight for land.

Women

The only women mentioned in Brazilian history books are queens, princesses, or mistresses. *Machismo* is still enshrined in Brazilian law: whereas a woman can be sent to prison for three years for having an abortion, and adultery is still a crime, rape is treated, not as an act of violence, but as a "crime against custom." Betrayed husbands still use "honor" as a defense for murdering their wives. But in other ways women's rights have advanced in the last ten years, since the 1988 constitution introduced equal rights and obligations for men and women, bringing Brazil into line with the most advanced European countries.

Women and Power

Twenty per cent of households are now headed by women, and more women have paid jobs than in any other Latin American country. In the professions, Brazilian women are everywhere. More women than men graduate from university; two-thirds of medical graduates and nearly half the law graduates are women. Even in engineering, a traditionally male career, a fifth of the graduates are now women. Pay has yet to catch up, however. Women still earn, on average, only just over half as much as men for doing the same job.

The Supreme Court is still all-male, but lower down the judicial pecking order, women judges have made most of the courageous decisions in recent legal history. Judge Denise Frossard became famous overnight for taking on the previously untouchable Rio gambling mafia and sentencing fourteen of their most notorious leaders to six years in jail. In politics, power remains firmly in male hands, with only a handful of women ministers, senators, and national deputies.

Outside Congress, 171 of Brazil's 5,000 towns and cities are now run by women. Between 1988 and 1992 the mayor of São Paulo, South America's largest city, was the Workers Party (PT)'s Luiza Erundina de Souza. Brazil's first-ever woman governor, the Liberal Front (PFL)'s Roseana Sarney, was elected for Maranhão in 1994. Two of the current five women senators overcame immense handicaps to get there. The triumphant progress of Benedita da Silva, a black Rio shanty-town dweller and former maid, has been an inspiration to many other black women. From the opposite end of the country 37-year-old Marina da Silva, a rubber-tapper's daughter who learnt to read and write when she was 14, and now has a university degree, provides another example of amazing perseverance. Both women belong to the PT.

Contraception and Fertility

Although women's groups have mushroomed, issues like contraception, abortion, and sterilization remain almost taboo in the press, largely thanks to the continuing influence of the conservative sector of the Catholic Church. The tradition of not allowing women to decide their own affairs goes back a long way. In the 1600s, convents were forbidden in Brazil because women were needed to increase the population, not shut themselves away and pray. At the end of the twentieth century, most Brazilian women still have no access to reliable information on contraception. Political parties of all persuasions wash their hands of responsibility, denying women's right to knowledge and access to safer alternatives.

Yet despite official inaction, the last fifty years have witnessed one of the world's most dramatic falls in the population growth rate. In 1940 a woman of childbearing age typically had over six children – by 1990 that figure had fallen to less than three. Resorting to mass sterilization, illegal abortion, and the pill sold over the counter without a prescription, Brazilian women have carried out, on their own, one of the most drastic population control programs in modern times. An estimated six to eight million women have been sterilized, fifteen per cent of them young girls aged between 15 and 24 years old. In contrast, only one per cent of Brazilian men have had vasectomies. Sterilization has also become popular because politicians offer it as a vote catcher during election campaigns, and some employers illegally demand proof of it to avoid the risk of having to pay maternity leave.

Women's Police Stations

A Brazilian invention, run entirely by and for women, the first women's police station opened in 1985 in São Paulo. The first day, three hundred women, many with visible cuts and bruises from their latest battering, queued up outside to register complaints. The policewomen had expected to deal with cases of rape by strangers, as well as domestic violence, but they found that most sexual abuse was committed inside the family by fathers, stepfathers, uncles, and brothers. Now there are 150 of the stations all over Brazil, and the idea has been adopted in other countries.

Children

Brazilians believe that children should be seen and heard, even in restaurants late at night. Children from wealthier families are often pampered, waited on by maids, chauffeured by mothers to and from after-school activities. Children tend to grow up less inhibited in a society where touch is not taboo and affection is openly expressed. Brazilians like children, except when they live on the street. Then they are perceived as a threat.

Films like *Pixote*, TV documentaries, and numerous books have told the world about Brazil's street children. Street children are not unique to Brazil. What is unique is that most of them expect to be killed before they are eighteen. Many of the killers are off-duty policemen involved in protection rackets and drug trafficking. Children are eliminated because they know too much or even if not already involved in crime, are seen as potential bandits. "I killed you because you didn't go to school and had no future," read a note left beside the body of nine-year-old Patricio Hilario, found in a Rio street in 1989. The National Movement of Street Children (MNMMR) says that ninety per cent of the murderers are never brought to justice. Ironi-

Street child in Recife *Paula Simas*

Selling sugar cane, Rio de Janeiro *Julio Etchart/ Reportage*

cally, a progressive Children's Act introduced in 1990 enshrined children's rights in law and introduced an innovative system of local children's councils. In Brazil, theory and practice are often distant relatives.

In 1993 eight children and adolescents were shot dead near the Candelaria church in the center of Rio. Juvenile court statistics show that in the three years since, over 3000 children aged eleven to seventeen died violent deaths in Rio, and the vast majority of them were murdered, by death squads, police, or other gangs. Because the Candelaria killings caused an international outcry, several policemen went on trial, creating a crack in the edifice of impunity which protects most killers.

Working Children

Children are driven onto the streets by the need to earn money as soon as they can beg or carry a tray of chewing gum around the cars at traffic lights. Now, in an attempt to prevent children taking to the streets, some local authorities have begun offering poor parents monthly payments for each child going regularly to school, to compensate for the income they would otherwise bring home.

Three and a half million Brazilian children work. In rural areas, poverty drives children into the cane fields and the charcoal ovens. In Pernambuco 60,000 children work as cane cutters. Ninety per cent start work between seven and thirteen, earning up to half their family's income. Obliged to use the same large machetes as the adults, over half have suffered accidents while cutting cane.

In Minas Gerais and Mato Grosso do Sul up to 6,500 children work with their families in primitive camps in the eucalyptus forests, producing charcoal for the giant steel companies in Belo Horizonte. Most have never been to school. The children feed the ovens with logs and later remove the red-hot charcoal, working in dense smoke and violent temperature changes. Their feet get burnt by the hot coals, their hands get splinters from the logs, their eyes are red from the smoke.

Four million children of school age are not in school. The current government of Fernando Henrique Cardoso has promised to outlaw child labor and make primary education a priority, raising the abysmally low wages of teachers. Some local authorities in the charcoal-producing areas and elsewhere have followed Brasília's example in paying low-income families a wage in exchange for them keeping their children at school.

Race

Brazil's patron saint, Nossa Senhora da Aparecida, is a black madonna and half of Brazil's 150 million people are black or mixed race, but official Brazil is white and TV commercials are positively Scandinavian. "Blacks only appear on TV as soccer players, suspects, or stiffs," complains one black activist. President Cardoso appointed the first ever black minister, footballer player Pelé. His soccer artistry dazzled the world but Pelé has always avoided the racial issue and never uses his prestige to attack prejudice.

Racism

Racial discrimination is illegal and offenders can be prosecuted, but few cases ever get to court. Discrimination is often too subtle, like the job adverts which ask for a "good appearance." Many blacks themselves are still ashamed of their color. When asked to describe themselves in the 1980 census, people came up with all sorts of euphemisms: "very sunburnt," "coffee-colored," "the color of caramel." Immigrants, adventurers, ex-Nazis, and runaway bank robbers have found more tolerance in Brazil than its own black citizens.

European and Japanese Immigration

People of European descent form the second-largest contingent. After the Portuguese, hundreds of thousands of Germans and Italian immigrants settled in the South. In Santa Catarina there are still German-speaking towns and villages. Blumenau's beer festival rivals Munich's, while São Paulo's pizzas owe nothing to those of Rome. Dutch, Poles, Swiss, Finns, and American Confederates have all created their own enclaves. In Espirito Santo, there is a higher than average incidence of skin cancer among the farmer descendants of Pomeranian immigrants who have intermarried and kept their very white skins.

Japanese immigration began in 1906, when the first boatload of second sons arrived, unable to inherit land in their own overcrowded country. Many soon fled the harsh conditions of the coffee estates and headed for the cities, especially São Paulo, which now has three-quarters of a million first, second, and third generation Japanese, making it the largest community outside Japan. They not only dominate the market gardening sector but have moved steadily up the social ladder. Yakotas, Uekis, Hanishoros, and Matsudas can be found in every area of business and politics. Wandering through São Paulo's Liberdade district, you might forget you are in South

America. All the shop signs are in Japanese (except for the occasional Chinese or Korean restaurant) and there are stores crammed with Japanese foodstuffs and locally-produced Japanese newspapers.

In the 1980s, Japanese immigration went into reverse as several hundred thousand children and grandchildren of Japanese immigrants left for Japan in search of a better life. They were disappointed to find that, although they looked Japanese and might even speak it, they were still treated as foreigners – their Brazilian lack of formality instantly gave them away.

Brazil has also seen an influx of Lebanese and Palestinians in the last twenty years, adding to its older Arab colony of Egyptians and Syrians. In the interior, where many Arabs used to work as traveling salesmen, they are confusingly called "*Turcos,*" Turks. Like the Jewish community, the Arabs have founded hospitals and clubs, and in Brazil, the two have been able to work together. Not so long ago, the president of the São Paulo stock market was an Arab, his vice-president a Jew.

The ease with which someone can disappear into the vast interior or the chaos of the huge cities has also encouraged less desirable immigrants. The infamous Nazi war criminal, Dr. Josef Mengele, spent twelve years in Brazil before he died, sheltered by Austrian sympathizers. Ronald Biggs, the English train robber, has lived peacefully in Rio for 21 years, exempt from deportation because he fathered a Brazilian child. Italian Mafiosi and Belgian mercenaries have all found it easy to blend into the cosmopolitan population.

Religion

The name of God is on everyone's lips in Brazil because of the ubiquitous catch-phrase "*Se Deus quiser,*" "God willing." "Inflation will be lower this month, God willing," says every Minister of Finance. "*Se Deus quiser*, I will get that bandit," swears the policeman, cradling his machine-gun. Few Brazilians would admit to being atheist, but their relations with God tend to be practical, rather than spiritual. Long-distance trucks sport hand-painted slogans invoking divine protection.

Churches like the Basilica of Brazil's patron saint, Aparecida, near São Paulo, are crammed with ex-votos, plaster casts of legs, hands, torsos, heads, whichever bit of the body was cured by divine intervention. On saints' days the roads are clogged with buses and trucks full of pilgrims going to "pay their promises" – give thanks for mercies received.

Once a year, hundreds of thousands of pilgrims crowd into the small Northeast town of Juazeiro, to give thanks for blessings received from Padre Cicero, a local priest and political leader excommunicated by the Church for performing miracles. Padre Cicero died many years ago, but remains far more popular than any saint canonized by the Vatican.

Statue of Christ, Rio de Janeiro *Paul Smith*

Rio's most famous landmark is the statue of Christ looking down over the city from Corcovado Mountain with his arms outstretched. Even the twentieth century concrete and glass palaces of Brasília have attracted their own brand of worshipers. Widely believed to be a city of cosmic forces due to its supposed location at the center of a magnetic field, in the nearby Valley of Dawn a mystic sect draws thousands of followers. The "Legion of Goodwill" has erected a pyramid there. Being a planned city, Brasília even has a special religious quarter, where temples, churches, and chapels of the different faiths co-exist side by side.

Rise of the Pentecostals

Brazil's 150 million people make it numerically the world's largest Catholic country, but the 500-year rule of the Roman Catholic Church is coming to an end, as Pentecostal Protestant churches spring up in converted cinemas and bingo halls across the country. Between 1990 and 1992, 710 new churches, five a week, were opening in Rio, ninety per cent of them Pentecostal. During the same period only one new Catholic church was consecrated.

The fastest-growing Pentecostal sect is the Universal Church of the Kingdom of God, led by self-styled Bishop Edir Macedo, a former lottery clerk.

In the days of high inflation, smartly dressed ushers raced up and down the aisles collecting sack-loads of money as worshipers dutifully paid their tithes and gave to special causes. Preachers told them that giving was the way to godliness. At the end of 1995, the Church was being investigated for fraud and charlatanism after a former preacher revealed the dubious methods used to extract more money from worshipers. Macedo has become a wealthy man, owning a fast-growing TV network and scores of radio stations. He is spreading his empire to many other countries in Latin America, Africa, Europe, and the U.S..

Catholic bishops recognize that the Pentecostals offer an attractive mix of emotion, participation, and faith healing. Some see them as something more sinister – a covert U.S. strategy to weaken the progressive Catholic Church and ease the way for neoliberal economic policies. But to people lost in the chaos and pressures of big city life the new churches seem to offer above all a moral code and a sense of self respect. Most of their preachers come from the same class and culture as their congregations, unlike the priests of the Catholic Church, many of whom, especially in the Amazon region, are foreigners.

Radical Catholicism

The spread of the evangelical Protestant Churches marks the end of Catholicism's monopoly and means that Brazil is becoming religiously pluralistic for the first time. It also means that the heyday of the Catholic Church's grassroots movement, the Comunidades Eclesiais de Base (CEBs), is over.

In the 1970s and 1980s, the CEBs were seen by some as the launchpad for a social revolution. They formed a key part of the reform movement that began within the Church in 1962 and deepened at the Bishops conference of 1968 in Medellín, Colombia, when the Latin American Church made an "option for the poor," based on the theories of liberation theology. Rejected by the conservative Church because it drew on Marxism, liberation theology inspired the practices of the CEBs.

The CEBs began as small neighborhood groups in rural areas or city slums who met to read the Bible, and discovered that what they read could be applied directly to their own lives. They spread rapidly all over Brazil, aided by the shortage of priests, which made the idea of laity-led groups more attractive to the Church. At their peak, they numbered 80,000 separate groups. During the military dictatorship (1964-85), the Catholic Church provided a sanctuary for the opposition movement – the only voice left for those without a voice and often the only place where trade unionists and human rights activists could meet in safety.

Base Christian Community, São Paulo *Paul Smith*

It did not begin like that. On the day of the coup, the bishops' conference gave thanks for Brazil's delivery from communism. But as the repressive nature of the regime became apparent, the bishops issued ever-stronger statements, criticizing torture, censorship, social injustice, and the lack of land reform, and calling for a return to Christianity.

As a result, churchmen and women became targets themselves. By 1979, 122 religious and 273 lay workers had been imprisoned, many of them tortured, and four priests had been murdered. The name of the outspoken Archbishop of Recife, Helder Câmara, was banned from mention in the press. In the Amazon, the bishop of São Félix do Araguaia, Pedro Casaldaliga, narrowly missed assassination because of his firm defense of the land rights of Indians and peasants. In Rio, the late Bishop of Nova Iguaçu, Adriano Hipólito, was kidnapped, stripped naked, and covered in red paint because of his "communism."

In São Paulo, Archbishop Paulo Evaristo Arns made his church a center of resistance to the military regime. There, he received and comforted the mothers of disappeared prisoners, wives of imprisoned strikers, tortured peasants, and refugees from other Latin American regimes. He was also sought out by multinational executives, military emissaries, and even, once or twice, by repentant torturers. When Jewish journalist Vladimir Herzog died as a result of torture, announced as suicide, Arns organized an ecumenical service which became an act of defiance towards the regime and the police and troops who had encircled the Cathedral.

The Church has also created new organizations to fight for social justice. CIMI, the Indian Missionary Council set up in 1972, and CPT, the Pastoral Land Commission founded in 1975, support and campaign for the Indians and landless peasants threatened by invasions, evictions, and violence. The various Justice and Peace Commissions defend human rights, and the Centro Santo Dias in São Paulo helps victims of police violence.

Decline of the CEBs

In 1985 the last military president, General João Figueiredo, handed over to a civilian president, José Sarney. The return of political parties, unions, and popular movements to center-stage left the Church without a clear political and social role.

In Rome, the new Pope, John Paul II, a conservative, had embarked on a campaign to tame the Brazilian Church, appointing conservative bishops to replace progressives and closing down seminaries that taught liberation theology. Cardinal Arns could not be removed, but the São Paulo archdiocese was divided up into five separate dioceses to reduce his power. In 1984 Brazil's leading liberation theologian, Franciscan friar Leonardo Boff, was summoned to Rome for an inquisition on his writing and banned from teaching or publishing for a year. He later gave up the priesthood.

African Religions

The African slaves brought their own gods with them, but since open worship was banned, they disguised them with Catholic names. So Ogum became St. George, Iansã became St. Barbara. The hybrid religions thrive today under their own names, candomblé, macumba, and umbanda. Candles burning at a crossroads or the headless body of a black hen are signs of a *trabalho*, an offering to the gods for something desired, or a curse on somebody. Whatever their religion, most Brazilians will treat such signs with respect.

In Bahia, which has Brazil's largest black population, candomblé priestesses have become well-known personalities, respected by political leaders. Syncretic practices, like the ceremony of washing the steps of the church of Nosso Senhor do Bonfim by candomblé followers, have become a regular tradition. On New Year's Eve, a million people of all religions pack the beaches of Rio to throw offerings into the sea for the goddess Iemanjá. Brazilians find no problem in keeping a foot in more than one church, selecting what they like from each different religion.

CANDOMBLE: RELIGION OF BLACK BRAZIL

Candomblé, the religion of the Yoruba nation of West Africa, arrived in Brazil aboard the slave ships. Banned from worshiping their own gods in a Catholic land, the slaves disguised them with Catholic identities: Ogum, the god of war, became St. George; Omolú, the god of healing, became St. Lazarus, and Iansã, goddess of winds and storms, became St. Barbara. The religious syncretism which resulted, also includes elements from indigenous beliefs. The cults involve animal sacrifices and offerings to the gods, accompanied by singing and drumming. In Bahia where candomblé is strongest, some priestesses (mães-de-santo) have become well-known public figures and candomblé ceremonies like the washing of the steps of the Bonfim church are part of the religious calendar.

Originally found only in the state of Bahia, Candomblé has spread throughout Brazil. Two believers, just initiated, enter the temple.
(Margreet Willemier Westra-Karten)

During the dance believers are possessed by Yoruba gods. A god greets believers in the temple by possessing and speaking through a spiritual medium.
(Margreet Willemier Westra-Karten)

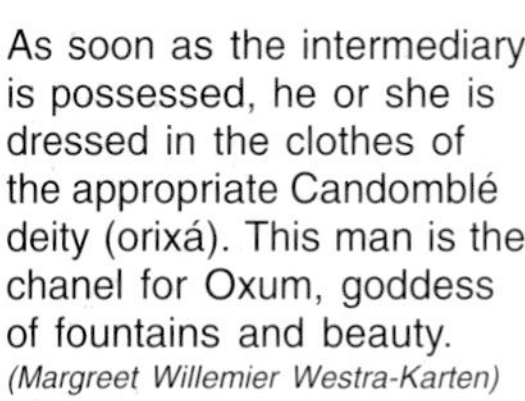

As soon as the intermediary is possessed, he or she is dressed in the clothes of the appropriate Candomblé deity (orixá). This man is the chanel for Oxum, goddess of fountains and beauty.
(Margreet Willemier Westra-Karten)

Oxóssi, the god of hunting, is also the commander of an army of Indians and is many times portrayed as a soldier. On the altar lie offerings of food, made to him by his disciples.
(Margreet Willemier Westra-Karten)

An Indian Orixá, Caipó, is seen here consuming a sacrificial bird. Caipó was already worshiped before the Portuguese arrived in Brazil.
(Margreet Willemier Westra-Karten)

This altar is devoted to the Exus, messengers of the gods associated with evil, who when bribed with food and drink, can be persuaded to answer requests for help.
(Margreet Willemier Westra-Karten)

The ghosts of dead children provide comic relief during the ceremonies. Possessing adults and children alike, they make jokes, jump around, eat sweets and drink lemonade, and scrounge money.
(Margreet Willemier Westra-Karten)

3 POLITICS

In just over a hundred years Brazil has been a monarchy, a republic, and a federation. It has been ruled by parliament, civilian presidents, military juntas, general-presidents, and by a civilian dictator. Being president of Brazil involves a certain degree of occupational hazard. In the last fifty years, one president has committed suicide, one resigned, one was impeached, another was overthrown by a coup, and one was taken fatally ill on the eve of taking office. Since 1955 only one elected president has completed his term of office.

Besides the plethora of presidents, there has been a surfeit of legislation. Since independence, seven constitutions have been approved or imposed. The latest, approved in 1988, is already being revised.

Two Brazils

Yet such constant changes only mask an unchanging, unwritten political system based on patronage and privilege. Through them all, the unofficial division of Brazilians into first- and second-class citizens has remained intact, leaving the ruling classes more secure and more economically successful than anywhere else in Latin America.

The huge gap between rich and poor has made the emergence of solid democratic institutions more difficult. Congress remains unrepresentative, with few members to defend the interests of the rural and the urban poor, black Brazilians, or indigenous communities, while hundreds of senators and deputies protect the property and purses of the wealthy. Brazil has never had a socialist or left-wing government, although members of left-wing parties have been ministers in coalition governments.

Weak Parties

Without strong parties, interest groups have taken precedence over ideologies, clientilism over the public interest. In Europe, class and religious conflicts gave rise to the first party systems, in the U.S. the presidential election system consolidated the American parties, but in Brazil, under the monarchy the small ruling elite stifled the formation of political parties which might escape its control. When the republic came, the executive joined forces with local oligarchies to maintain power by preventing the rise of independent parties. Fraud was easier without strong opposition.

So while other Latin American countries have for generations had their *Blancos* and *Colorados*, their *Liberales* and *Conservadores*, in Brazil parties appear and disappear overnight. In the last Congress, members changed parties 200 times during its four-year term. In 1995 eighteen parties were represented in Congress, out of thirty which fought the last elections.

This fragmentation of the parties has slowed the work of Congress, as each bill has to be painstakingly negotiated not only with each party, but with each of its separate factions. Instead of representing an ideological position, most parties have become agglomerations of politicians representing regional, class, corporate, business, or individual interests. The *ruralistas*, representing farming and agribusiness, are one of the most powerful lobbies, with over 120 votes. The Amazon Bloc brings together 90 mostly conservative, anti-environmental, anti-Indian congressmen and women from the nine Amazon states.

The over-representation of conservative interests was increased and made permanent in a piece of gerrymandering by General-President Ernesto Geisel in 1977, after a vote had failed to go his way. As a result, each congressperson from São Paulo currently represents 467,000 inhabitants, while one from the small northern state of Roraima represents only 30,000, skewing power in favor of the right-wing representatives from the interior.

Political Parties

PMDB: The Brazilian Democratic Movement was set up during the military regime to be the official opposition party and maintain the fiction of a democracy. It evolved into a real opposition and in 1985 formed the government under the first civilian president, President José Sarney. It still commands many votes, but ideologically it is a rainbow coalition which can vote in any way.

PSDB: The Brazilian Social Democrat Party, also called the Tucano party after its symbol, a toucan, was created in l989 by center-left dissidents from the PMDB, including current President Fernando Henrique Cardoso. Like the toucan, the PSDB is top-heavy. It has big names but lacks votes and so ended up adopting a neoliberal economic program and allying with the conservative PFL in order to win the 1994 presidential election.

PFL: The Liberal Front Party, launched in l984 by a group of dissidents who wanted to distance themselves from the unpopular pro-military PDS party, has managed to stay in power by offering votes and financial support to more charismatic candidates from other parties. Strongest in the more backward northeast states, it now forms part of the ruling coalition with the PSDB.

PT: The Workers Party, founded in l979 by a group of trade union leaders and intellectuals, is the only ideological political party. After two defeats in presidential elections, in 1995 its charismatic president Luis Inácio Lula da Silva stood down as leader. The party is split internally between a hard-line left-wing and a more social democrat faction. It has slowly increased its congressional representation, and has elected two state governors and several city mayors.

The Return to Democracy

Brazil moved from authoritarian regime to a politically free society without rupture, bloodshed, show trials, or purges, but it has paid the price. The extraordinarily drawn-out transition period gave time for numerous politicians to abandon ship, disengaging themselves from the unpopular military and presenting themselves instead as the opposition, where they vigorously resisted pressure for more radical reforms.

In 1984 a Congress still intimidated by the generals voted to maintain the indirect system of presidential elections, despite a campaign that had brought unprecedented millions on to the streets clamoring for the right to choose their own president.

Playboy President

When they at last regained that right in 1989, Brazilians voted for Fernando Collor, an arrogant young outsider whose glamorous image dazzled much of the electorate, tired of dour generals and elderly politicos. Supported by the powerful TV Globo network, Collor used an array of dirty tricks to overtake the PT's Luis Inácio Lula da Silva at the last moment. Collor wowed the population with his playboy lifestyle, his mastery of the sound-bite (*"I'll kill inflation with one karate chop"*) and his ambitious promises to modernize Brazil, bring it into the First World, smash corruption and streamline the government.

His first drastic anti-inflation measure, the confiscation of almost all of the nation's savings for eighteen months, brought ruin to many people and plunged the economy into recession. Fidel Castro, in Brazil for Collor's inauguration, commented, "Even I wouldn't have dared do that." Collor reduced import barriers and opened up the economy, but inflation surfaced again and in 1992 his own brother, Pedro Collor, accused him of corruption. A congressional inquiry decided he had misused his public office and after mass demonstrations, Collor resigned, as Congress was about to vote for his impeachment.

Fernando Collor, disgraced former president

Julio Etchart/ Reportage

Fernando Henrique Cardoso

Collor was succeeded by Itamar Franco, a mediocre politician chosen as vice-president exactly because he would never overshadow his charismatic boss. Franco

Fernando Henrique Cardoso AP

was honest but unpredictable. Although something of a populist, he chose as his Finance Minister the former sociologist Fernando Henrique Cardoso, who was determined to introduce a market economy. Cardoso became in effect Franco's prime minister, running the economy and the government, but by now he had his own political ambitions.

After the high drama of Collor's presidency, Franco provided an easy-going interregnum in which the economy grew and Brazil won the 1994 World Cup. But inflation began to spiral, reaching nearly fifty per cent a month in May 1994. Four months before the presidential elections, the Real Plan was introduced, choking off inflation and successfully stabilizing the economy, but with a much higher cost of living.

After years of grappling with bundles of banknotes and calculating in thousands and millions and seeing prices rise every day, suddenly life became much simpler. Prices stayed the same and Brazilians had more money in their pockets. The PT's Lula had been leading all the way in the election campaign, but the Real Plan's rush of feel-good factor won the day for Cardoso.

The Plan sparked a consumer boom, as the return of hire purchase enabled people to buy consumer durables on credit. To keep prices down, the government reduced import duties and Brazilian streets crowded for decades with locally-built Fords, GMs, and Volkswagens were suddenly full of imported BMWs, Mercedes, and Hondas.

Cardoso was popular with many different groups. An intelligent, cosmopolitan man who looked and sounded good, his promises of constitutional reforms to denationalize state sectors and deregulate the economy were welcomed by foreign investors, bankers, and governments as a return to sensible government after ten years of roller-coasting. In Brazil, the establishment felt safe because of his alliance with the PFL, while progressives felt that he would honor his intellectual past and his campaign pledges by introducing social reforms.

However, Cardoso failed to capitalize on this goodwill and after a year in government had achieved little in the way of lasting reform. His hopes of rising above the old habit of exchanging favors for votes had proved misplaced. With so many parties to deal with, confusion reigned and important votes went the wrong way. "The government needs a leader just to deal with the fifteen party leaders it has to negotiate with," joked José Genuíno Neto, a PT deputy.

On the social front, the government was slow to act. In an unguarded moment Communications Minister Sérgio Motta complained that "sociological masturbation" was delaying action. The only new social initiative was the "*Comunidade Solidária,*" modeled on Mexico's Solidarity program. Run by Cardoso's anthropologist wife, Ruth, it directed government grants and food to needy communities.

Record interest rates were introduced to kill off the consumer boom and damp down the risk of inflation, but only at the cost of rising unemployment. A million people in São Paulo alone were jobless at the end of the year.

Grassroots Movements

Modeled on the state-controlled unions of Italian Fascism in the 1930s, emasculated into welfare centers by the military in the 1960s, only in the 1980s did the trade unions begin to recover their independence and combativity. The new phase began in 1978, when 120,000 workers in the car industry in São Paulo's industrial zone defied the ban on strikes, downed tools, and packed the small football stadium at Vila Euclides to listen to the fiery oratory of an unknown young union leader, Luis Inácio da Silva, known simply as Lula. Despite police harassment and tear-gas attacks, the strike was victorious, turning Lula into a national figure and establishing the São Bernardo Metalworkers Union as the heart of the new union movement.

In 1983, defying the government ban on union organizations that included different trades, the Central Unica dos Trabalhadores, CUT, was created. It included both urban and rural workers from all over Brazil. CUT soon became Latin America's largest trade union organization with 15 million affiliated members, although millions of Brazilians in unregistered jobs continue to be unrepresented by any union. To weaken the influence of the left-wing CUT, the government encouraged the creation of a rival organization, the Força Sindical, led by a former communist, Luis Antonio Medeiros.

Lula, the PT's charismatic leader

Julio Etchart/ Reportage

At the same time that the unions were beginning to flex their muscles, other popular movements began to appear. In 1977 church groups began a protest at the cost of living and persuaded a million people to sign a petition. The cost of living movement subsequently evolved into numerous local organizations, such as the *favelados* (shanty-town dwellers) and the *sem teto* (homeless). Many maintained close links with the progressive Catholic Church, drawing members from radical Base Christian Communities and support from radical priests and nuns. Their meetings were often held in church halls. In the 1980s, national movements of street children and the *sem terra* (landless) also grew up.

With their promise of empowerment and change and the threat they pose to the status quo, the popular movements are looked on with mistrust and suspicion by many of Brazil's more affluent citizens. They are routinely branded as violent and criminal whenever they show signs of being well organized or successful. In the mid-1980s, over 200 plots of waste land in São Paulo's East Zone were invaded by groups of "sem teto" unable to afford rising rents. Some of the squatters' camps were destroyed after battles with the police in which one man was killed and many injured, but others won the right to stay. The Workers Party mayor, Luiza Erundina de Souza, who was elected in 1988, began a self-help building scheme with the "sem teto." Over 10,000 families benefited but her successor, right winger Paulo Maluf, suspended the scheme, claiming financial irregularities.

A Land Occupation

April 1, 1995: Under the cover of darkness over a hundred buses and coaches approach the Arco Iris cattle ranch in the Pontal do Paranapanema, 500 miles west of São Paulo. The vehicles are packed with landless peasant families and their household belongings. Soon black-plastic-roofed shacks are dotted over the empty fields, stoves and beds are quickly installed inside, and committees are set up to organize water, food, sports, and schools.

The squatters cut the wire fences and the next day, tractors are plowing up the fields for planting. With military precision, the Sem Terra Movement (MST) has organized another land invasion. Eighteen hundred families are now camped there, hoping that soon a piece of these empty pastures will be theirs. Then they will plant food and feed their families instead of living in favelas, where they must get up at three or four in the morning to travel out to the big farms to cut cane or pick fruit for starvation wages.

Landless Movement

The Sem Terra Movement (MST) began in 1984 when, tired of official promises, a group of rural activists decided that land reform for Brazil's 4.5 million landless families would only come through direct action. With the slogan "Occupy, resist, and produce" they began seizing large estates all

MST members blessing each other with soil from newly occupied land during a religious service

Paul Smith

over Brazil. Each target was carefully studied beforehand to make sure it would fit the legal definition of unproductive and so be eligible for expropriation by the government under Brazil's land legislation.

Since then, more than 22 million acres have been expropriated by the government, the owners compensated, and 131,000 families settled. At the beginning of 1995, a further 17,000 families were squatting in 45 camps all over Brazil, some at the roadside, some inside invaded areas, all waiting for official expropriation. Some squatters have occupied the same patch of land ten or twenty times, each time being evicted by police, before the government has finally agreed to expropriate the land and hand it over.

Not all the newly-settled areas have succeeded. Denied technical assistance or credit, some have failed, forcing new settlers to abandoned their hard-won land. But thousands of former sharecroppers, tenant farmers, and migrant workers have been transformed into productive small farmers, often working their land cooperatively. A 1991 survey by the UN's Food and Agriculture Organization (FAO) showed that average incomes in these settlements were three times higher than the minimum wage and productivity was above average. Some even export their produce.

Unlike other popular movements, the MST has deliberately chosen a collective form of leadership to avoid providing targets for assassination. New generations of leaders are constantly being trained. The movement's success has prompted accusations that it is running secret training camps where guerrilla tactics are taught. In fact, while the MST's broader aim is to create a socialist state, and Che and Mao posters can be seen in MST offices, its heroes include national historical figures such as Zumbi and Antonio Conselheiro. In São Paulo's Pontal region, leaders have been arrested on charges of forming a criminal gang.

At a national level, genuine land reform has been promised by every president since 1964, but the powerful landowners" lobby has always blocked any serious attempt, either in Congress or through bloodshed. In the first two years of the Cardoso government there were two massacres of "sem terra."

In 1995 in Corumbiara, in the Amazon state of Rondônia, police surrounded 600 families who had occupied a ranch before dawn and ten people, including a seven-year-old child, were shot dead. Two policemen also died. In April 1996 in Eldorado do Carajás, Pará state, police fired on a group who were on a protest march to the city of Belém, killing nineteem men. In both cases the police were accused of executing men who had already been detained, local ranchers were alleged to have paid off the police and in spite of the outcry, police destroyed evidence to hamper investigations.

Campaign Against Hunger

In recent years, one of the most prominent grassroots movements has been the Campaign Against Hunger, launched by one man in 1993 and spreading rapidly to create over 5000 committees at its high point, spread across Brazil. The original idea was simply to bring food to as many as possible of the 32 million Brazilian families officially classified as poor. Since then it has moved on to creating jobs, training, and campaigning for land reform.

The Campaign's founder and inspiration is a man sometimes compared to Gandhi. Herbert de Souza, universally known as Betinho, is thin and fragile, an HIV-positive hemophiliac whose amazing drive and energy enable him to cut through red tape and recruit the rich and famous to the socially acceptable cause of feeding the hungry and providing jobs. Campaign committees, set up in schools, churches, neighborhoods, and banks, have provided the impetus for hundreds of self-help projects in shanty-towns and poor communities, from vegetable gardens to computer classes and waste recycling.

4 THE ECONOMY

As the plane flies into São Paulo, first-time visitors to Brazil cannot believe their eyes. Stretching away to the horizon is the biggest concentration of skyscrapers on the planet. Overshadowed by the more glamorous Rio, São Paulo's sheer size is breathtaking. With 17 million people, (second only to Mexico City in world terms), São Paulo is the locomotive that drives Brazil, accounting for half of its economic output. São Paulo is the industrial and banking center; it is where the PT and the CUT began; it is the part of Brazil that reminds you that the country is the world's tenth largest industrial economy, a major supplier of food to the world and one of the top ten arms manufacturers.

At night the city's cosmopolitan heart pulsates with a hundred different rhythms from tango to techno, and the aromas of thousands of *cantinas*, *churrascarias*, pizza palaces, Chinese restaurants, bars, and bakeries mingle in the air. But at every traffic light there is a reminder of how Brazil's wealth is built on poverty, as hordes of adults and children descend on waiting cars to sell chewing gum, flowers, biscuits, or fruit. Over a million people in São Paulo live in favelas, over three million live in *cortiços*, the overcrowded tenements where ten or more families share a single bathroom.

Boom and Bust

"Everything that is planted here, grows," Pedro Alvares Cabral wrote home ecstatically in 1500. Like the other European colonies, Brazil's role was to be plundered for the enrichment of the mother country. At different times in the ensuing 500 years, Brazilian products have dominated world trade, providing raw materials such as sugar, coffee, rubber, and gold that became essential to the way of life of the developed world.

During the gold boom in the seventeenth century, Brazilians (excluding the slaves) had the highest per capita income in the world. Brazil has always been a rich country, but its wealth has remained in the hands of the few. Little has been shared with those who helped to create it.

The first Brazilian export, the redwood used to make a dye much in demand in Europe, set the pattern. For 30 years after discovery, 300 tons a year were exported until the accessible wood was exhausted and trade declined. Today mahogany is being furiously logged to supply the world's demand and by the year 2000 there will be little left.

Sugar and Gold

For 400 years the Brazilian economy was dominated by successive single product cycles of boom and bust. After redwood came sugar, its master and slave system leaving a legacy that still shapes Brazilian society today. "King Sugar" produced over half of all export earnings during the entire colonial period. Then came gold. Brazil's gold rush lasted only a hundred years, but during that time Brazilian gold accounted for half the total production of all the Spanish and Portuguese colonies.

In the seventeenth century, Brazil was the world's greatest gold producer and the capital city symbolically moved south from Salvador, near the sugar-cane fields of the Northeast, to Rio, close to the gold mines of Minas Gerais. Brazil became the engine of Portugal's economy, its gold paying for imports of British manufactured goods. In this way, Brazilian gold helped finance England's Industrial Revolution, but in Brazil itself the Portuguese monarchy banned industrial development, so that all available manpower would be available for agriculture and mining.

Coffee

After sugar and gold came coffee. Coffee may seem as Brazilian as football and Carnival, but it is an imported plant, first brought to Brazil from French Guiana in 1727 by a certain Sergeant Palheta. The climate and soil in the South around Rio, São Paulo, and much later, Paraná, proved ideal for coffee. By the 1900s, Brazil was the world's major producer and coffee remained its leading export from 1831 to 1973. Immigrants rapidly replaced slaves on the coffee plantations – in one twenty-year period from 1879 to 1899, nearly one million immigrants settled in São Paulo state.

Whereas sugar had concentrated wealth in a few hands, coffee helped to spread it. Coffee, unlike sugar, did not need plantations but could be grown by smallholders. Neither was it a monopoly crop: beans and cereals could be grown between the rows of trees. Coffee brought development: railroads and ports had to be built to transport it overseas to the consumer markets of the North. Santos, on the São Paulo coast, is still Brazil's biggest port, though now it exports cars and machinery as well as coffee and fruit. Coffee wealth paid for elegant country houses furnished with the best that Europe had to offer, and large mansions began to appear in the small provincial town of São Paulo, turning it into Brazil's main financial center. Money brought industry and political power in its wake.

At the end of the nineteenth century came the shortest of all Brazil's commodity cycles, rubber. The bicycle and the motorcar had appeared and the U.S.A and Europe clamored for rubber to make pneumatic tires. Manaus, the Amazon capital, briefly became the wealthiest city in Brazil as fortunes

Coffee harvest in Minas Gerais *Tony Morrison/ South American Pictures*

were made from the latex collected by enslaved Indians. The rubber boom was cut short when plantation rubber from Malaya and Ceylon began to swamp the market, grown from saplings smuggled out of the Amazon by an Englishman. Wild Brazilian rubber's share of the world trade fell from 90 per cent in 1910 to two per cent in 1937.

Before and after independence, the British had dominated Brazil and the other Latin American economies, finding them doubly useful as suppliers of essential raw materials and markets for the products of the mills and factories that mushroomed with Britain's industrial revolution. But by the Second World War, the U.S. had replaced Britain as its dominant trading partner, supplying half of Brazil's imports and taking 40 per cent of its exports.

Industrialization

In the 1940s, President Getúlio Vargas laid the foundations of Brazil's postwar industrial boom by creating giant state steel and oil companies and nationalizing Brazil's twenty private railways.

Between 1950 and 1980, first under elected governments and then under military rule, Brazil's economy enjoyed an average growth rate of seven per cent, one of the longest periods of sustained high growth in world history. In a far cry from today's free market fashions, the government subsidized and directed private sector activity, whether local or foreign.

State-led industrialization and import substitution led to rapid urbanization. Within 30 years Brazil was transformed from a largely rural society into a country where three-quarters of the population lived in towns and cities. A large workforce was needed for the new factories being set up by companies from Europe and the U.S. to produce cars, TV sets, and domestic appliances, attracted by tax incentives of all sorts. Even so, the job supply failed to keep up with demand, as millions of impoverished peasants flocked to the cities in search of the new jobs.

The corporations dominated the private sector, producing consumer goods, while the military concentrated on developing their own missiles, planes, armored cars, and weapons, swiftly turning Brazil into a major arms exporter. The middle classes soon developed the same consumer expectations as their peers in the U.S. and Europe, because economic policies, especially under the military, increased income concentration at the expense of the poor.

Rising Debts

Foreign loans poured into Brazil, as Western bankers rushed to offload their surplus dollars regardless of the long-term viability of the projects they were financing. Whether going to state or private companies, the repayment of these loans, at floating interest rates, was guaranteed by the government. Foreign debt was nothing new. On independence in 1822, Brazil already owed over £3 million to the London banks. The Brazilian economic miracle was loquaciously admired by First World bankers and politicians, who preferred to remain silent about the embarrassing underbelly of the regime – the torture, censorship, and repression being exposed by human rights organizations.

Brazil's "miracle" was finally destroyed by the military's disastrous response to the oil shocks of the 1970s. The steep rise in oil prices meant that Brazil, an oil importer, was suddenly faced with a greatly increased oil bill and a resulting trade deficit. Unwilling to admit the country's difficulties because they would reflect on the success of military rule, President Ernesto Geisel, the fourth general to rule the country since the coup in 1964, reacted with imperial disdain. Brazil, he declared, was an island of tranquillity and recession was unnecessary. Instead Brazil simply borrowed more dollars to cover the trade deficit, adding to the debt being run up by Eletrobras, the state energy utility, and the other state companies involved in the military's ambitious infrastructure program of nuclear power stations, giant dams, roads, railroads and a petrochemical complex.

Enter the IMF

Crisis turned into disaster when the second oil shock of 1979 was followed by a dramatic rise in U.S. interest rates. The military and government technocrats refused to seek rescheduling of the snowballing foreign debt, which had grown from $12.6 billion in 1973 at the beginning of the oil crisis to $64.2 billion by 1980. They delayed because rescheduling would involve accepting an International Monetary Fund (IMF) austerity package, and this might affect government candidates' chances in the November 1982 governorship elections.

In the event, they lost out on both counts. The opposition won in all the major states and Brazil was virtually bankrupt, having used up all its foreign reserves. The government had no choice but to go, cap in hand, to the IMF. Between 1983 and 1985 Brazil submitted seven letters of intent to the IMF, promising free market reforms in return for a partial debt bail-out. Brazil had the economic clout to impose more reasonable terms and even set up a debtors cartel to negotiate jointly with the banks, a prospect much feared in Washington and Frankfurt, but the generals and technocrats buckled under and paid up, despite the cost to Brazilians in the shape of recession and savage cuts in social programs.

Economic Stagnation

The government failed to meet its IMF targets on spending cuts and other measures, but kept up its debt repayments. Economic stagnation followed as Brazil added dollars to its long list of exports to the First World. By 1985, when the 21-year-old military regime finally handed over power to a civilian government, inflation was on the rise and the country was in the worst recession since the Depression of the 1920s.

Free of the generals, wage strikes took off and inflation spiraled to nearly twenty per cent a month. President José Sarney responded by introducing the Cruzado Plan, freezing wages and prices and changing the currency, the first of many attempts over the next ten years to stabilize the economy.

Brazil began a ten-year cycle of rising inflation, change of finance minister, wage and price freeze, new currency, a brief respite, then back to rising inflation. Between 1986 and 1994, the government got through eight finance ministers, seven stability plans, and six currencies. In 1987, a moratorium on foreign debt payments was belatedly declared, supported with nationalist fervor by the president of Congress, Ulisses Guimarães, an outspoken opponent of the military regime, who declared, "The debt is a hemorrhage, bleeding the country to death."

But Finance Minister Dilson Funaro's pilgrimage to Western capitals to plead for a debt reduction was met with scorn by hard-faced bankers, indifferent both to the human cost of the capital outflow and to the individual tragedy of Funaro, a man whose missionary zeal was inspired by the knowledge that he did not have long to live because of cancer. Despite the repayments, Brazil's total debt rose relentlessly, almost doubling to reach $123.4 billion by 1990.

Brazil remains the Third World's largest debtor, second only to the United States in world terms. In 1994, with the debt standing at nearly $150 billion, Finance Minister Fernando Henrique Cardoso finally reached agree-

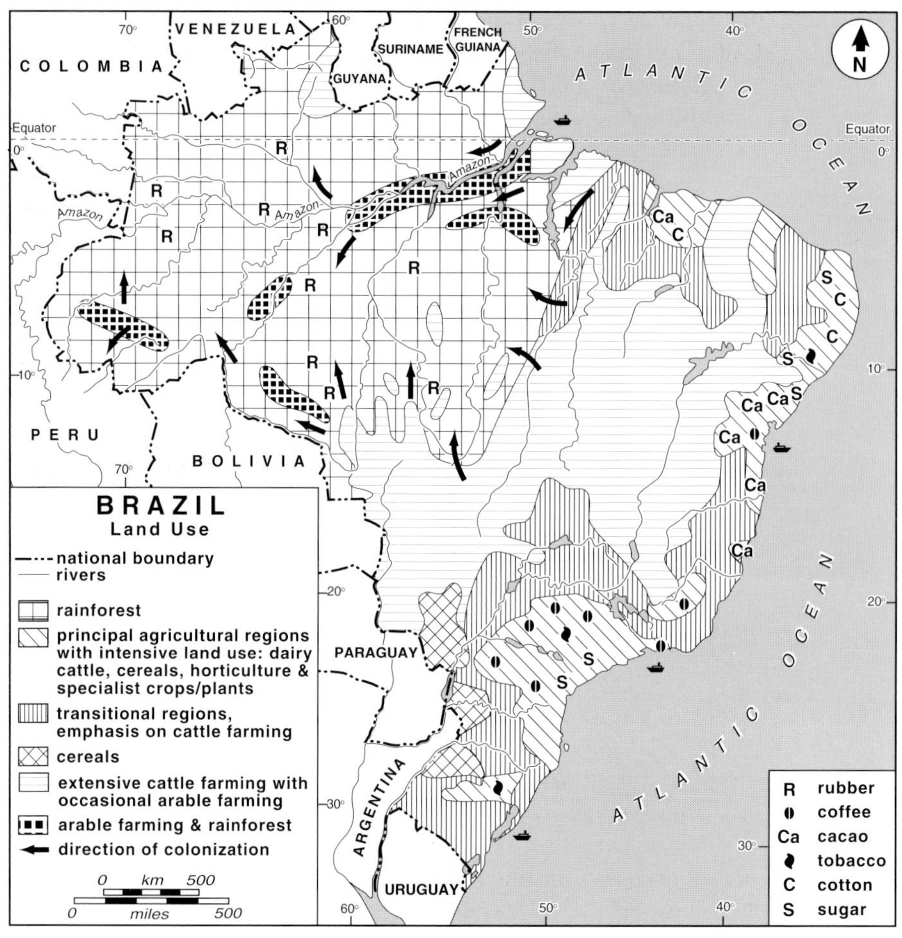

ment with the banks. Repayments reached $21.7 billion in 1995, $20 billion in 1996. With a gross domestic product close to $700 billion, the payments do not represent the huge burden they do in some smaller countries. Nevertheless, they mean billions of dollars less for social programs, which is where cuts are inevitably made.

Unleashing the Market

The election of the inexperienced Fernando Collor in 1989 began a new phase in Brazilian economic policy. Collor wanted to drag Brazil helter-skelter into the First World by liberalizing the economy and shrinking the state sector. "Better to be the last country in the industrialized world than the first of the developing countries," he claimed. On his first day in office, Collor froze private assets and savings, plunging the economy into chaos. Thousands were ruined overnight; some committed suicide.

In the rush to deregulate, efficient and essential government agencies were abolished along with the inefficient and unnecessary, aggravating the chaos. In 1992 Collor resigned just as Congress approved his impeachment for corruption and was succeeded by vice president Itamar Franco who continued to privatize and open up the economy.

Brazil's extremely high interest rates and low priced utility shares soon had it classified as an attractive "emerging market." The projected privatization of giant state companies like Petrobras (oil), Telebras (telecommunications), Eletrobras (electricity), and the São Paulo state gas, water, and energy companies had investors rubbing their hands. But after a year of the Cardoso government, the necessary constitutional reforms were still held up by a Congress determined to wring every possible concession in exchange for their votes. Investor enthusiasm began to wane.

Real Plan

In 1994 Cardoso was elected on the back of the success of the Real Plan, an economic stabilization program which he had introduced as Itamar Franco's Finance Minister. Introduced on July 1, when inflation was nearing 50 per cent a month, the plan's success depended on freezing wages and ending indexation, once prices had been allowed to rise to a peak. The plan also involved the biggest currency switch ever carried out in any country, as the new *Real* replaced the *cruzeiro* and billions of banknotes and coins had to be distributed throughout the vast country.

Brazil then enjoyed an unprecedented period of low inflation, down to single figures throughout 1995 and into 1996, boosting Cardoso's popularity. But in 1996 concern began to grown about soaring unemployment figures of over fifteen per cent in São Paulo and over 30 per cent in Recife. Industry was undercut by cheap imports and being battered by some of the highest interest rates in the world, as the government sought to keep inflation down and attract foreign capital into the country.

Inequality

Brazil is now the world's tenth largest industrial economy, with a gross domestic product of almost $700 billion, far ahead of every other developing country except China, yet the income gap within its borders is widening. Not only have the rich increased their share of the national income, but a World Bank study has shown that the rich even receive a larger slice of government social spending. The top twenty per cent of the population

A *favela* in Vila Prudente, eastern São Paulo *Paul Smith*

receive the benefits of 21 per cent of government spending, while the poorest twenty per cent get only fifteen per cent.

Private hospitals, for example, most of them profit-making, were allocated 62 per cent of the Ministry of Health's budget for hospital care in 1995, while public hospitals received only 38 per cent. At the same time, the funds for preventive medicine were cut back, including nutritional programs which help the poor most. Experts say that Brazil's spending on social programs would be adequate if it were targeted specifically at the 24 million people who live below the poverty line.

It has been left to local governments to show that important improvements can be achieved at little cost. When Brasília's governor, Cristóvam Buarque, decided to pay out a monthly allowance of $100 to nearly 15,000 low-income families, in return for them keeping their children at school instead of sending them out to work, the measure took just 0.6 per cent of the capital's budget. By attending school more regularly, the children perform better, and subsequently have a chance of getting better jobs than their parents, breaking the cycle of poverty that traps future generations.

5 AMAZON AND ENVIRONMENT

For those used to the Thames or the Potomac, the vastness of the Amazon is difficult to grasp. Rising in the Andes, flowing into the Atlantic, the 3,800 mile-long Amazon is the longest river in the world. The river basin, two-thirds of it in Brazil, drains an area as big as the United States, excluding Alaska. Seventeen of its tributaries are over 1,000 miles long. Five hundred miles upriver from the sea, the mouth of one of these tributaries, the Tapajós, is twelve miles across. Marajó, the island that lies in the mouth of the Amazon, is larger than Denmark. Two thousand different species of fish live in the Amazon basin, which covers one twentieth of the world's surface and contains a fifth of its fresh water.

The rainforest proper covers 1.5 million square miles, and just one acre may contain up to 179 species of tree. The average for temperate forests is six. The Amazon rainforest contains the planet's largest gene reserve, its greatest store of biodiversity, a pharmaceutical cornucopia. Gold, uranium, bauxite, manganese, cassiterite, oil, and gas have been found in the subsoil. The rainforest does not cover all the Amazon basin: there are also savannah, valleys, and mountains, including Brazil's highest mountain, the Pico da Neblina. As destruction advances at the fringes, there are now millions of acres of cleared forest used for cattle pasture and farming.

Utopian myths: a "tiger hunt" in the rainforest

Myths and Legends

A fertile source of myths and legends of lost explorers, giant sloths, and amorous dolphins, the Amazon has always attracted explorers, adventurers, and eccentrics. Its fantastic size has inspired equally fantastic plans to dominate it, all of them eventually defeated by the conditions that have also earned it the title "Green Hell." Henry Ford tried to tame the wild rubber tree into growing in plantations: he planted three million neat rows of trees at Fordlandia on the edge of the Tapajós river, only to see them wiped out by a fungus. In the 1960s, the Hudson Institute in the U.S. proposed damming the Amazon to turn it into a series of great lakes.

In 1967 American billionaire Daniel Ludwig bought 4 million acres of rainforest at less than $1 an acre in the state of Amapá. He cleared the forest and planted imported species such as the fast-growing *gmelina* and California pine to provide wood for a pulp factory, which he had towed across the world from Japan. Many of the trees died. He brought Dutch engineers to build polders for rice paddies, but the rice did not flourish. He built a railroad, hundreds of miles of roads, and a model company town, while across the river 15,000 laborers and prostitutes squeezed into the Beiradão, a waterside favela. After spending an estimated $3 billion, Ludwig gave up and pulled out. Only the wood-pulp factory remains in business.

Conquering the Amazon

The idea of penetrating the forest with railways or roads has always appealed. At the end of the nineteenth century, when the rubber boom was at its peak, first the British, then the Americans, planned a railroad to bring Bolivian rubber through Brazil to Belém on the Atlantic coast. The British gave up, the Americans succeeded. Twentey-two thousand men, recruited from all over the world, worked on the 200 mile-long track connecting the Mamoré and Madeira Rivers, which finally opened in 1912, just as the rubber boom was collapsing. Over 6,000 men died from malaria, yellow fever, dysentery, and other diseases during the five years it took to build the aptly-named Devil's Railway. In 1971, after years of decline, the railway was finally closed and the engines sold off as scrap.

The dream of conquering the Amazon remained. In 1972, sixty years after the ill-fated Madeira-Mamoré was opened, the Brazilian military decided it was time to link the Atlantic and Pacific Oceans, via the Amazon. The generals wanted to integrate the "empty" Amazon region with the rest of the country, easing social tensions in other regions by shipping off landless farmers to occupy its empty lands. The "wilderness" would then become a profitable productive area of export agriculture.

Finance Minister Delfim Neto talked of conquering a new country within the Brazilian nation and called on businessmen to carry out the definitive conquest of the Amazon. The Transamazon Highway was presented as the solution to the drought that was devastating the Northeast. The "people without land," the drought victims, would be transferred to the "land without people" and installed in agrovilas, purpose-built settlements strung out along the new road.

Manaus harbor on the Amazon *Julio Etchart/Reportage*

Critics feared it would merely be linking a dry desert to a humid wilderness, but machines began bulldozing the red earth road through the dense trees. Families were airlifted to their new homes in the forest. Today much of the road has been washed away by the heavy rains, and most of the families have abandoned the land where they were dumped and then forgotten.

The state of Rondônia was set aside as a solution for the small farmers of the south, driven off their land by hydroelectric dams and soybean farms. In a modern-day equivalent of America's nineteenth-century wagon trails, hundreds of thousands of families set out on buses and trucks to travel two thousand miles north, and settle on the subsidized plots supplied by the government. Between 1970 and 1980, Rondônia's population multiplied tenfold. The military regime also offered tax incentives to big companies, multinational corporations, and banks to set up cattle ranches.

By 1977, 336 agricultural projects in the Amazon basin region had been approved for funding by SUDAM, the government development agency. Seventy per cent of their investments was covered by the public purse. A network of over a hundred hydroelectric dams was planned to provide energy: heavily subsidized electricity was offered to giant aluminum projects set up on the coast.

A sharecropper clears a patch of Amazon rainforest *Julio Etchart/Reportage*

In 1980 another ambitious development project, Greater Carajás, was launched. An 18 billion-ton iron ore mountain had been discovered in the Eastern Amazon. Delfim Neto said the iron ore would be enough to "pay off the foreign debt," which then stood at $60 billion. By 1995, not only was it not paid off, it had doubled to $160 billion.

Infrastructure for the project included a 550 mile-long railroad to carry the ore to the port in São Luis. When it was announced, the heavily subsidized Greater Carajás project promised jobs and prosperity to a region where thousands of rural workers and landless peasants lived in poverty. Yet outside the model company town which houses the employees of the state-owned Vale do Rio Doce Company, ragged families of charcoal-burners still live in miserable huts at the side of the road, and the forest has been razed and burnt to make way for cattle.

In 1994 the military unveiled a new megaproject for the Amazon. The Air Force wanted to buy a $1.4 billion U.S.-manufactured radar system to monitor air traffic in a region which has become a drug-traffickers paradise. Defenders of the project suggested it could also be used to detect invasions of indigenous and ecological reserves. President Cardoso was a keen supporter of the project, known as Sivam, although a police bug on a diplomat's phone revealed a tangled web of corruption, influence peddling, and CIA involvement in the scheme.

The latest plans to develop the Amazon region put the emphasis on eco-tourism, including a jungle monorail, floating hotels for 30,000 visitors and a 100-feet-high statue in the middle of the river at Manaus, proposed by the flamboyant governor of Amazonas state, Amazonino Mendes, who has a reputation for outlandish ideas. The Manaus Opera House has been lovingly restored to all its former splendor for the 1996 centenary.

Environment

In 1972 the Brazilian delegation famously informed the Stockholm Environment Conference that development was more important than pollution. Twenty years later, Brazil hosted the 1992 Earth Summit and was able to show off a whole infrastructure of specialized agencies for protecting the environment, from a special ministry down to state and municipal secretariats. There is even a new breed of "environmental prosecutors" who take both state and private companies to court for crimes of pollution and contamination, while the 1988 constitution introduced a five-year deadline for the demarcation of indigenous reserves and the need for environmental impact reports before new development or industrial projects could go ahead.

Theory and Practice

But good legislation is little use when political will is lacking. The environment secretary of the Amazon state of Roraima in 1994 was a well-known mining entrepreneur; in the town of Itaituba, at the heart of the Tapajós gold-mining area, the municipal environment secretary in 1993 was the owner of a clandestine mining camp; a recent environment minister, Henrique Brandao Cavalcanti, included two loggers in Brazil's delegation to an international congress on protected species to lobby against the inclusion of mahogany.

In the run-up to the Earth Summit, the G-7 group of developed industrial countries came up with a Pilot Plan for Tropical Forests. They promised $1.5 billion for environmental protection, including the demarcation of Indian reserves and conservation parks. Compared with other Latin American and European countries, Brazil has few protected areas: only 1.8 per cent of its total area, compared with 15 per cent in Venezuela, 8 per cent in Colombia or 5.5 per cent in Holland.

Not only the Amazon is at risk. According to the World Wide Fund for Nature, "the rapid occupation of territory and the absence of a policy of creating conservation areas makes the protection of important ecosystems like the Atlantic Forest and the Cerrados doubtful." Less than one per cent

Pollution at a gold mine in the Amazon state of Pará

Julio Etchart/Reportage

of the Atlantic Forest's area is protected, while 80 per cent is in private hands. The Cerrados – the vast plateau of central Brazil – loses eight million acres of open land to agriculture each year.

Mining and Logging

In the Amazon region itself, the invasion of Indian and ecological reserves continues by loggers and garimpeiros who contaminate Amazon rivers with the mercury illegally used in gold-panning. Studies show mercury contamination of riverside and Indian populations, who eat the fish from rivers used by the garimpeiros. Almost all the mercury is imported from Europe for other purposes and smuggled up to the Amazon where it is freely sold in pharmacies and stores.

Logging is now probably the greatest threat to the rainforest. To reach the scattered mahogany trees, hundreds of miles of dirt tracks are illegally cut through the forest. Trucks loaded with giant tree trunks lurch down them on their way to the sawmills, now scattered in thousands throughout the Amazon region. Floating carpets of trunks destined eventually for the furniture shops of London, Tokyo, and New York cover stretches of river.

Under pressure from boycott campaigns, British timber importers have tried to ensure they buy only legally-logged wood, but face a whole system of falsified documents and fraudulent certificates issued by corrupt officials at IBAMA, the government's environmental agency. As a result, illegal logging of mahogany from Indian and ecological reserves continues apace. A proposed road to give Brazil a Pacific outlet through Peru, via the state of Acre, is condemned by environmentalists because it will bring the diminishing mahogany stands much nearer to the Japanese market. Asian loggers, having exhausted their own forests, have moved into Brazil's northern neighbors, Guyana and Surinam, and have begun to buy up logging companies in Brazil.

The huge forest fires of the late 1980s, when tracts of rainforest were burnt for cattle pasture, covering the region in a heavy pall of smoke and ash, slowed in the early 1990s, but the government's space research institute, INPE, has recorded a substantial rise in the burning since 1994. The amount of rainforest already destroyed is nearly twelve per cent.

Defending the Forest

The environmental cost of Amazon dams like Tucuruí, Brazil's largest national dam, and Balbina, built in the early 1980s, was initially ignored, but in 1989 protests by the well-organized Kayapó Indians forced the suspension of the proposed Monte Belo dam on the Xingu river. The dam-building program was then largely shelved for lack of funds.

In the 1980s, Chico Mendes, a trade union organizer in Acre, led rubber tappers in collective actions known as *empates* to stop cattle ranchers felling the forest which contained their livelihood. In December 1988 he was shot dead by a cattle-rancher's son. His murder made him an international environmental "eco-martyr" and the government felt obliged to implement Mendes' proposals for environmentally sustainable "extractive reserves" for the rubber tappers. Unfortunately, the abysmally low price of wild rubber has since forced many tappers to leave for the towns.

Concrete Jungles

For most Brazilians, the Amazon is as remote as Siberia and urban pollution is their main environmental concern. Since the Real Plan was introduced in 1994, and gas became relatively cheap, traffic on the streets of Rio and São Paulo has increased by over twenty per cent. So far, city authorities have failed to come up with any solution, except to build more tunnels and bridges.

Success in Curitiba

Yet Brazil has one city, Curitiba, which has become a byword for environmental innovation. The city's fame began with Jaime Lerner, an architect who served three terms as Curitiba's mayor. The secrets of the city's success are ingredients rarely found elsewhere in Brazil today – long-term planning, administrative continuity, and a belief that rich and poor are entitled to the same high standard of public service.

Instead of expressways for private motorcars, Curitiba has created a fast-moving and cheap public transportation system, which has attracted nearly a third of the city's rush-hour motorists, so reducing air pollution levels. The city has doubled in size since the 1970s, but most favelas have basic infrastructure, and recyclable waste can be exchanged for fresh food, school books, and even Easter eggs. Neighborhood centers, open 24 hours, have brought government departments nearer to people, while new parks, cultural centers, and pedestrian precincts mean that the city now has 50 square yards of green space per inhabitant compared to São Paulo's 12 square yards.

While the quality of life has been improving in Curitiba, it has steadily deteriorated in most of Brazil's cities. The Tietê and the Pinheiros rivers that divide São Paulo are narrow and unglamorous, unlike the breathtaking Bay of Guanabara which encircles Rio de Janeiro. Yet both are heavily polluted – the rivers with industrial sewage, the bay with oil and detritus from the ships in Rio's port. Internationally-financed projects to clean up the waters are now under way.

Struggles in Cubatão

Some hope is offered by the experience of Cubatão, the industrial complex near Santos which belched out so many tons of polluting particles from its petrochemical and steel plants that the region became known as the Valley of Death. In Cubatão, pollution got so bad that some doctors claimed that babies were being born without brains in the nearby town of Vila Parisi. In 1983, after an emergency shut-down when levels got dangerously high, Governor Franco Montoro invested in a pollution control program which successfully reduced particle emissions.

The environmental prosecutors of Cubatão also won a victory in court, obliging the French multinational Rhône Poulenc, which for years had dumped toxic waste in the region, to pay compensation. In 1995, in an effort to reduce air pollution from the city's three million vehicles, the state environmental secretary, Fabio Feldman, proposed that motorists should only use their cars on alternate days, but the mayor, Paulo Maluf, refused to cooperate. "Traffic jams mean progress," he explained without conscious irony.

6 CULTURE

Carnival

The Rio Carnival is the biggest song and dance spectacle in the world, with a strong element of Roman circus as the rich and the famous, ministers, presidents, sports stars, film idols, tycoons, bankers, and playboys banquet and booze the night away in luxurious boxes overlooking the *Sambodromo*, the purpose-built parade ground where the samba schools perform.

Down below, hour after hour, to the hypnotic and deafening beat of hundreds of drummers and percussion players, thousands of exuberantly dressed dancers twirl, gyrate, leap, and sway. The TV cameras focus on the near-naked women, but each school has up to 3000 sambistas dressed in rich costumes of plumes, sequins, and satins. It is hard to believe that once Carnival is over, the eighteenth century courtiers, Amazon Indians, African warriors, and Egyptian pharaohs will metamorphose back into maids, bus drivers, laborers, shop assistants and garbage collectors.

The samba schools began in the favelas and still draw most of their members from one locality. Celebrities, TV stars, models or soccer players are invited to "appear" with the school, and increasingly middle-class Brazilians and even tourists buy themselves a Carnival experience, their less-than-expert samba steps mercifully hidden in the general melee.

Behind the four-day parade lie months of rehearsals and an extraordinary amount of research into each school's theme, often used to satirize historical or current events. The 1994 winner, Imperatriz Leopoldinense, dug up a little known century-old episode, when Pedro II decided to import camels to cope with the drought in the Northeast. The camels succumbed, while the local donkeys survived, allowing an ironic reflection on the superiority of the underrated homegrown product.

The satire sometimes becomes surreal – where else would torture become a Carnival theme? Yet a few years ago the Santa Cruz school, celebrating the 25th anniversary of the satirical newspaper *Pasquim*, a fervent critic of the military regime, produced a float with gigantic torture instruments. Around the float danced 25 dwarfs dressed as generals.

The conservative archbishop of Rio, Dom Eugenio Sales, has frequently criticized the excesses of Carnival. On one occasion, he took out a court injunction to stop a replica of the Corcovado Christ being put on a float. The answer of Joãosinho Trinta, one of Rio's most famous and creative *carnavalescos*, was to wrap it up in black plastic so that nobody could see it, although everyone knew what it was. It was Trinta who coined a phrase that became famous in answer to criticisms of the extravagant luxury of his floats and costumes: "Intellectuals like poverty, the people want luxury."

Capoeira, a combination of dance and martial art born out of slavery *Julio Etchart/Reportage*

As Carnival has grown and attracted live coverage by the major TV channels, so commercial interests have become more intrusive. Advertising by Brazil's two major beer companies is everywhere. For all that, one of the great delights of the Rio Carnival is still the juxtaposition of the ordinary and the fantastic, the sight of a group of Roman legionnaires going home by bus, or a couple of the older women clambering into a car in their vast crinolines.

Music

Brazilian music is much more than samba. In the 1960s, Tom Jobim's hit tune *The Girl from Ipanema* turned bossa nova into a global sensation; in the 1980s it was the turn of the sensual lambada to storm clubs around the world. Bahia, home of Brazil's largest black population, has thrown up generations of creative singers, composers and musicians, including singer-composers like Caetano Veloso, his sister Maria Betania, Gilberto Gil, and Gal Costa, with their warm, melodious voices singing of love, poverty and protest.

Today they are joined by all-black bands such as Olodum and Timbalada and composers like Carlinhos Brown. In a country where so few people read, music is an important form of communication; most of Brazil's radio and TV commercials are sung, each political party has a theme tune at election time, and in the Northeast, *repentistas* make up instant ballads about current events, full of innuendo and irony.

During the dictatorship, the military insisted that the lyrics of all new songs had to be submitted to the censors and some were banned from performance. Nevertheless, *Caminhando* (Walking), by Geraldo Vandré became the anthem of the resistance movement, while everyone realized that Chico Buarque's apparently innocent *Apesar de Você (In spite of you, there must be another day)* referred to the military. Elis Regina's *O Bebado e o Equilibrista* (*The Drunk and the Tightrope Walker)*, which referred to well-known exiles, became another opposition favorite.

In Rio Grande do Sul, the revival of regional pride in the 1980s led to a spurt of music festivals where singers and musicians abandoned rock and pop and began singing forgotten gaúcho songs and composing new ones.

Literature

Brazil cannot claim any writer with the universal prestige of Colombia's Gabriel García Márquez. The book that has sold best abroad, *Beyond All Pity*, is not the work of a famous writer, but the diary of a black woman, Carolina Maria de Jesus, describing her tough daily life in a São Paulo favela. She died a few years ago, ignored and penniless.

The literary prestige of at least one nineteenth century writer, however, is growing fast. Joaquim Maria Machado de Assis (1839-1908) is now hailed as one of the most important contributors to Portuguese literature. Setting his novels in the Rio of the mid-1800s, he described the intimate details of daily life, class conflict, and the corrosion of institutions in a decaying, slave-owning, patriarchal society.

Of mixed blood and humble background, Machado de Assis has been described as the most profound interpreter of the dying days of Brazil's Empire. His best known works are *Memórias Póstumas de Bras Cubas, (Epitaph of a Small Winner), Dom Casmurro* and *Quincas Borba (Philosopher or Dog).* Another classic of the nineteenth century was Euclides da Cunha's *Os Sertões (Rebellion in the Backlands*), describing the war to destroy Canudos. Sent to cover the military campaign against the rebels by a Rio newspaper, da Cunha shared the prejudice of the time against the rebels, who he portrayed as ignorant religious fanatics, but also revealed the brutality of the upholders of law and order.

Search for Identity

In 1922 a Week of Modern Art held to commemorate 100 years of independence became a landmark event, launching a search for a distinctive

Brazilian identity to replace the prevailing Eurocentrism of art and politics. Indian and black culture were rediscovered and the dehumanization of the modern industrial world rejected. Out went waltzes and polkas, in came the samba. Erudite composer Heitor Villa-Lobos wove Brazilian rhythms into his music and created the famous *Bacchianas Brasílianas*. Candido Portinari painted scenes from the plantations, the docks, and the drought. Jorge Amado, a communist whose books became popular on both sides of the Iron Curtain, described the harsh life of the cacao plantations of Bahia, while Érico Veríssimo portrayed the cruelty and bloodshed of the separatist wars in Rio Grande do Sul.

Sociologist Gilberto Freyre wrote *Casa Grande e Senzala* (*The Masters and the Slaves)*. Although Freyre's theory of benevolent master-slave relations has been widely rejected, he helped to make the idea of miscegenation (racial mixing) more acceptable by extolling its advantages. In 1928 Mario de Andrade wrote *Macunaíma*, the story of an anti-hero. Based on a legend of the Makuxi Indians, *Macunaíma* is an outrageous, amoral survivor who lives on his wits and so was seen as a fitting hero for modern Brazilians. For some, the book was also the first example of what was to become Latin America's most successful literary export, magical realism.

Cinema

Although it has one of the largest cinema audiences in the world, Brazil's own film industry has struggled to establish itself, winning just 50 international awards in nearly 100 years of film-making. In the 1960s, the *Cinema Nôvo* (New Cinema) directors Glauber Rocha and Ruy Guerra won acclaim with films that mixed religious fervor and social realism like *O Pagador de Promessas* and *Deus e o Diabo na Terra do Sol*, but they then fell victim to censorship under the military regime.

During the 1970s and 1980s, when political films were banned, the state film agency Embrafilme ended up funding mostly soft porn and children's films. In 1990 President Collor closed down Embrafilme and the film industry collapsed, but in 1995 with the introduction of tax breaks for companies who backed films, a revival began.

Architecture

Past, present, and future are all to be found within a few hours of each other in Brazil. The city of today is São Paulo, incessantly tearing down the past and building yet more sophisticated skyscrapers, road tunnels and shopping malls, while the tenacious favela dwellers cling to every bit of empty land, no matter how steep, risky, or cramped.

Only ten hours away by road is Ouro Preto, a hillside town of steep, cobbled streets and baroque churches built of soapstone, still essentially the

The Prophet Oseas, by Aleijadinho, Congonhas

Tony Morrison/ South American Pictures

same as in its heyday during the eighteenth century gold rush. Here, Tiradentes and the other rebels conspired against the Portuguese monarchy, while Aleijadinho, the half-caste son of a slave, left his inspired mark on hundreds of church carvings and statues in and around Ouro Preto. Crippled by leprosy, his tools had to be tied to his mutilated hands.

Brasília

Another six hours by road from Ouro Preto is the city of the future, Brasília, Brazil's third capital, a brand new city built in empty scrubland which now has well over a million inhabitants. The brainchild of President Juscelino Kubitschek, the city was planned by Lúcio Costa in the shape of an airplane fuselage.

But the man most associated with Brasília is architect Oscar Niemeyer, universally recognized as one of the great names of modern architecture. Born in 1907 and a life-long communist, Niemeyer designed many well-known buildings abroad, but it was the innovative architecture of Brasília, with its curves, ramps, and columns that made his international reputation. For André Malraux "the only columns comparable in beauty to the Greek columns are those of the [presidential palace of the] Palace of Alvorada."

Niemeyer wanted the new capital to be "the act of affirmation of an entire people." This philosophical concept took priority over the functional aspects of the buildings, to the future discomfort of its eventual more prosaic users – diplomats, civil servants, and congressmen and women. He wanted Brasília to be a democratic city where rich and poor would share the advantages of a planned, healthy environment. "Brasília was the proposal for a country which never was, created during the only moment of faith in itself which we've experienced in recent years," observed the poet Ferreira Gullar.

Instead, Brasília repeated the pattern of Brazil's older cities. The poor were expelled from the center to the periphery, in this case satellite towns, some of them 30 miles away. When the military took power, the Three Powers Square, where Executive, Congress, and Judiciary faced each other on equal terms, was disfigured by the erection of a giant flagstaff, a symbolic reminder of where power really lay.

Football

Every sort of sport is practiced in Brazil. If you look hard enough you can find old Italians playing *boche* (bowls), third generation Japanese playing baseball, and even the odd game of cricket at the British clubs in São Paulo and Rio. But there is only one game that counts: soccer, as essential a part of the Brazilian identity as samba and black beans.

It is hard to believe that when soccer was first played in Brazil it was derided as "the funny English game," a foreign transplant that would never catch on, more suitable for the well-nourished Anglo-Saxons than the less athletic Brazilians. One short-sighted commentator wrote, "It is like borrowed clothes that do not fit. For a foreign custom to establish itself in another country it must be in harmony with the people's way of life and fill a gap, and we already have the corn straw ball game...."

Soccer first came to Brazil in 1894, when Charles Miller, the Brazilian-born son of British parents, returned from school in England with a couple of footballs and a set of rules in his steamer trunk. It went on to become the national passion. Miller's daughter, still alive, says proudly "My father brought joy to Brazil." Intense joy, on the four times when Brazil won the World Cup, the last in 1994, but also intense anguish, when it failed. In 1950 the World Cup final was being played in Rio's famous Maracanã stadium before a capacity 150,000 crowd. An easy victory for Brazil against tiny Uruguay was a foregone conclusion, so when Uruguay unexpectedly scored to win, a deathly silence fell on the giant stadium. People wept with disbelief, men had heart attacks, and some committed suicide. Forty years later the unfortunate Brazilian goalkeeper is still haunted by that terrible moment.

The King

There have been generations of brilliant players. Pelé, real name Edson Arantes do Nascimento, is probably the best-known soccer player of all time, scoring over a thousand goals during his professional career. In 1995 President Fernando Henrique Cardoso chose Pelé, who has often admitted to cherishing political ambitions but always avoided the race issue, as Minister of Sport. Known as *O Rei* (The King), Pelé visited South Africa at the same time as Britain's Queen Elizabeth. When President Nelson Mandela reportedly rescheduled the Queen's program to fit in a meeting with Pelé, Brazilian papers had their headline ready: "The King overshadows Queen's visit."

The passion for football has made fortunes and political careers. During the military regime, giant stadiums were built in many cities. The national championship grew bloated as second-rate clubs were promoted to favor

Passion of the people: fans at the Flamengo v. Fluminense soccer derby in Rio's Maracanã stadium

Julio Etchart/Reportage

local political supporters. Election candidates still donate club gear to local teams in exchange for votes.

But using soccer as an opium for the people has sometimes backfired. During an international match in Paris in 1978, TV cameras could not help showing the giant banners unfurled by Brazilians in the crowd calling for an amnesty for political prisoners, while famous soccer players, like Socrates, have campaigned for the Workers Party. Corruption scandals are frequent, involving rigged games and bribed referees. Many of the clubs and federations have been run by the same officials for decades. Known as "*cartolas*" – literally "top hats" – these officials enjoy immense power and prestige and have become wealthy men.

The national passion has also claimed its share of victims. In 1989 the pilot of a commercial airliner on a routine flight in the Amazon was so engrossed in listening to the Brazil v. Chile match in Rio that he failed to notice he was flying south instead of north. When the plane ran out of fuel it crashed in dense rainforest and was only found three days later. Luckily, most of the passengers survived.

Motor racing

Only motor racing has come anywhere near the popularity of soccer, but interest has waned since Ayrton Senna's tragic death on the Imola track in 1994. In the last twenty years, Brazil has produced two other Formula One champions, Emerson Fittipaldi and Nelson Piquet. Three times Grand Prix champion Senna was mourned like a national hero. On the day of his funeral, São Paulo came to a standstill as over two million people turned out to line the route and say farewell to their idol, buried with all the honors of a head of state.

Gambling

On almost every street corner, a man sits at a small table, or leans against the wall of a bar. He merges in with the other sidewalk habitués: the fruit-seller, the popcorn man, the lame beggar, the car-washer, the lottery ticket seller. During the day a steady stream of people come up to him, and he writes numbers down on slips of paper. Money discreetly changes hands. If you get close enough, you might hear the words "butterfly" or "lion." For this is Brazil's mysterious, clandestine *jogo do bicho*, the animal game.

It all began a hundred years ago, when the owner of the Rio Zoo ran out of money to feed the animals and started a raffle to raise funds. The winner had to choose the right animal. It soon became a craze and the Zoo was packed out, not with animal lovers, but with gamblers. The game grew so popular that it spread to the streets and all over the country. The authorities attempted without success to ban the new national obsession. It is said that 60,000 people work for the jogo do bicho in Rio alone and the annual turnover is put at $2 billion.

The game is now more sophisticated but is still based on 25 animals and the total honesty of the bookies, as no receipts are given. The jogo do bicho has become part of Brazilian culture – anyone who dreams about snakes or monkeys knows they must bet on that particular animal.

Mafia Connections

What for millions is just an innocent flutter also has its more sinister side. Jogo de bicho is run by a mafia and the bosses, known as *bicheiros*, have become powerful men accused of involvement in crime and drugs. Being patrons of the popular jogo do bicho means they can present themselves as benevolent members of society, masking their criminal activities by sponsoring samba schools and local soccer teams.

The law has traditionally been unable or unwilling to tackle them, but in 1994 a judge broke through their protective shield of bribery and corruption and sentenced fourteen of the bosses to six year sentences for forming an armed gang. Even so, the press soon reported that their cells were equipped with color TVs and hi-fis, they received visitors for barbecues and birthday parties, and continued to conduct their deals on mobile phones.

Media

Illiteracy is dropping, but twenty per cent of adult Brazilians are still unable to read and write, and up to 60 per cent can do little more than write their own name. As a result, newspapers are read by a tiny minority and most people get their news, opinions, ideas, and prejudices from commercial television and radio.

One network, Globo TV, has dominated the airwaves for decades and been the mouthpiece of every government, military or civilian. Presidential pronouncements are always timed to precede the main evening Globo news – even its competitors arrange their schedules around it. The Globo TV network covers 99 per cent of Brazilian territory, and until recently claimed audiences of nearly 80 per cent. Seventy-five per cent of Brazilian TV's media advertising budget goes to Globo, while TV's total share of the national advertising budget is 50 per cent (compared to about twenty per cent in the U.S.).

Internationally, TV Globo ranks fourth amongst the world's television networks, with almost as many employees as the BBC. But alongside its size and sophistication are the idiosyncrasies of a family firm. Like Alfred Hitchcock appearing in his own films, Globo's aging president, Roberto Marinho, likes to feature in his own newscasts, receiving awards or decorations, and writes moralistic editorials to be read at the end of the news.

Marinho has been a power behind the throne of every recent president, and has been accused innumerable times of slanting the news to favor the government. But during the worst excesses of the military regime, even TV Globo had to obey the yard-long official telexes, listing all the subjects that must not be mentioned to avoid jeopardizing national security.

TV Globo has sold its fast-moving, often humorous, sometimes satirical, but always sexy soap operas around the world. Its costume soaps top the ratings in China and Cuba with the story of Isaura, a white girl brought up as a slave, transforming actress Lucélia Santos into a star better known in those countries than in Brazil. After 30 years of dominating audience ratings, Globo's stranglehold is now under threat from other commercial channels such as SBT, Manchete, Record and Bandeirantes.

Although TV and radio concessions are free, they carry no public service obligations. That is left to the impoverished state TV channels. Globo does, however, transmit supplementary school courses for young adults and used to have an excellent children's program. The Cardoso government plans to tap the huge potential of TV and video for educational purposes.

Traditionally, governments have awarded TV and radio concessions in reward for political services. In 1988 President José Sarney bought himself

Bahiana woman selling snacks, Salvador

Tony Morrison/South American Pictures

an extra year in office by distributing hundreds of new TV and radio concessions. Virtual licenses to print money because of the advertising revenue, they are also invaluable aids to winning elections.

Food and Drink

Centuries of growing sugar-cane has given Brazilians a sweet tooth. The ubiquitous *cafezinho* – small black coffee – invariably comes steeped in sugar. Sugar-cane rum, or *pinga,* is drunk neat but the delicious *caipirinha*, an aperitif, adds sugar, lemon, and ice to the rum. The result is widespread tooth decay and millions of people who have lost all their teeth before they are middle aged.

Brazilian cuisine is rich, varied, and tasty. The national dish, *feijoada*, a black bean stew, was invented by slaves who had to make do with the left-over bits of pig, the trotters, tail, and ears, while their masters feasted off the prime cuts. The result is a tasty, if heavy, dish eaten with manioc flour, a slice of orange, and rice. Restaurants serve feijoada only on Wednesdays and Saturdays. Manioc (cassava) flour is a staple all over the North, where it accompanies freshwater fish, and in the Northeast, where it is eaten with *carne do sol*, dried meat.

In Bahia, where the slave population outnumbered the white, regional dishes are heavily influenced by African traditions and dendê palm oil is widely used. In Rio Grande do Sul, the eating habits of the original Indian population have been preserved, but made sophisticated. The *churrasco*, barbecued meat, is no longer cooked on spits stuck in a hole in the ground but roasted on electrically rotated spits. Up-market apartments include their own barbecue room. The *chimarrão* (mate tea) is still drunk from a gourd through a silver-plated siphon, but these days the boiling water comes from a thermos flask.

Guaraná, an Amazon fruit used as a stimulant, can now be found in pills and capsules in health shops all over the world. In the Amazon it is sold in a hard stick which should then be grated with the dried tongue of the *pirarucu* fish and mixed with water.

BRAZIL IN 2000

Economics and Politics

At the beginning of the third millennium, economic and social inequality remains Brazil's defining factor, with the gap between rich and poor in Brazil still the largest in the western hemisphere. Approximately 17.4 % of Brazil's 170 million people live below the poverty line. Average life expectancy for a Brazilian male is only 63 years, for a woman, 71 years.

The *Real* Plan (see page 51) faced its biggest challenge in 1998, as the world financial crisis caused investors to panic. When Russia defaulted on its debt in August 1998, the shock waves were felt as far as Brazil, forcing the country to hike annual interest rates to the unprecedented level of 50% per year, in a bid to stem capital flight which amounted to almost $30 billion between August and September 1998 alone. On the other hand, a major achievement in 1998 was the reduction of inflation to its lowest level in the past 50 years (2.5%).

It was largely the success of the *Real* Plan in bringing the first stability in prices Brazilians had known for years that caused Fernando Henrique Cardoso to be re-elected to a second term in office in October 1998. However, there was widespread political and social opposition to the cuts in the government's budget demanded by the IMF to support the country through the crisis. Cardoso managed to push through the austerity measures required by the IMF and in November was the recipient of a $41.5 billion IMF-led international bailout program in an attempt to keep investment in the country. With the 8th largest economy in the world, Brazil was seen to be the last defense against an international economic meltdown.

However, it was Brazilians who paid the price for international stability. The cost of maintaining the *Real* at its artificially overrated value against the dollar has been soaring unemployment, thousands of bankruptcies among companies and factories and gigantic deficits in balance of payments and internal debt. The crisis was brought to head by the governor of the state of Minas Gerais, ex-President Itamar Franco, who declared a moratorium on debt repayment. The government could no longer contain the crisis and it culminated in a 40% devaluation of the *Real* in January 1999.

Corruption scandals continued to erupt, involving politicians at all levels and also top-ranking policemen. The latest involved the Mayor of São Paulo, Celso Pitta, whose estranged wife accused him of bribing city councillors to vote against an investigation of his financial transactions, and of making personal profit out of his administration. The term of Pitta – who was a political unknown before being launched by his former boss and mayoral predecessor, rightwing populist Paulo Maluf – saw a worsening of the city's already serious problems. Traffic pollution and congestion grew, while education and health services, which received diminishing investments, deteriorated.

A congressional criminal prosecution investigation launched in 1999 to look into drugs and organised crime was very successful in exposing mayors, deputies, congressmen and policemen involved in drug trafficking, torture and murder. Many arrests were made. Although the investigation's results are lauded by the majority of Brazilians, it has also exposed the extent to which the drug trafficking and organized crime has penetrated Brazilian society at all levels.

New Technology

Brazil has embraced new technology enthusiastically. There has been a dramatic mushrooming of mobile phones and internet users and the internet domain .br is the second largest in Latin America, after .ar (Argentina). The commercial battle for free access to the internet has arrived in Brazil and the country has become the epicenter of the fight among internet companies to position themselves in Latin America. Brazil ranks 7th in the world among internet users (before France, China, or Spain) and at the end of 1999 had an estimated 6.8 million internet users.

While in some areas Brazil is among the leaders in modern technology, in social indicators it continues to hold a significantly low position on the list of the United Nations Human Development Index – in 1999 it was 63rd. Meanwhile, the 20 biggest landowners own more land between them than the 3.3 million small farmers. There are riches to be made for those who have access to land and foreign markets: Brazil remains the world's largest producer of coffee and the second largest producer of soya beans and sugarcane. Overall, Brazil is the world's third largest exporter of food.

It is the issue of access to land and land reform which has inspired what has been called "the most important social movement in the world" — the growth of the Movimento dos Trabalhadores Rurais Sem Terra (MST). Its membership is estimated to be as high as 1.2 million. Thousands of activists have participated in occupations of idle land, building temporary and permanent camps and settlements, establishing schools and running farm cooperatives. New communities founded by the MST can be found all over Brazil, although many of them struggle to survive because of cuts in government funding for family agriculture.

"Brazil 500 Years"

The year 2000 was the 500th anniversary of the "discovery" of Brazil by the Portuguese. As in 1992, when the 500th anniversary of Columbus' first voyage to the Americas was commemorated, Brazil's official celebrations were not endorsed by many people, particularly the indigenous communities.

The high point of the official celebrations was the arrival of a flotilla from Portugal, including a replica of Pedro Alvares Cabral's ship on the anniversary of the "discovery" – April 22. The ship was met at Coroa Vermelha beach by the Presidents of Brazil and Portugal and a range of dignataries. Officially Brazil was commemorating "the meeting of two civilizations" – which, according to the comment published in *Jornal do Brasil* by the Portuguese writer and Nobel Prize winner Jose Saramago is like celebrating the encounter of German and Jewish cultures during the Second World War.

The official events were criticized for their triumphalist tone and for their insensitivity. The government decided to build a Museum of Discovery in Coroa Vermelha, clearing away a Pataxo indigenous village to make room for it, while re-housing the Indians in small pseudo-Indian huts without running water. The official organizing committee did not include any indigenous people. The Pataxo Indians who live in the area are still persecuted and attacked by local ranchers who have been given their land, and on a recent occasion, when the Pataxo tried to retake the land, a school bus was burned, Indians physically attacked and their leaders arrested.

A counter event to mark the 500th anniversary was prepared by indigenous groups, black organizations and the MST called "The Other 500" (*Os Outros 500*). It included a *"Marcha Indigena"* of 2000 indigenous peoples from all over Brazil. The aim of the Other 500 is to draw attention to the situation of the indigenous population after 500 years of massacres, invasions, slavery and neglect, as well as seeking recognition for the wealth of cultures and experiences which make up modern Brazil, including the significant contribution made by the country's African heritage.

A few days before the marchers arrived at the coast, local police destroyed a monument placed by indigenous communities near the official cross erected to mark the anniversary, in a gratuitous demonstration of lack of respect for the descendants of Brazil's original inhabitants. The 500 year anniversary provoked discussion about Brazil's racial mix, about racial democracy amid discrimination against the black population who make up more than half of the population.

Environment

The environment in Brazil is not only about the loss of the Amazon rainforest, the issue that so galvanized the international environmental community in the 1990s. Whether it is pollution from traffic in São Paulo, or the deplorable state of Rio's beaches, or the announcement that all life in Rio de Janeiro's Lagoa Rodrigo de Freitas, an inland lagoon, is dead, Brazil has its share of work to do in cleaning up its environment.

In Amazonia, figures for forest deforestation and devastation from fire continue to betray environmental loss on a massive scale. Between 1994 and 1995 the rate of loss of forest in the Brazilian Amazon doubled. In 1998, 17,000 square miles were deforested, more than double what government official sources reported – 7,000 acres of rainforest were destroyed by one cattle rancher alone. To date, approximately 16 per cent of the Brazilian Amazon has been destroyed for short-term profit. Friends of the Earth commented that the figures had "potentially disastrous implications for global climate change and species loss." In 1998, vast forest fires in northern Brazil destroyed up to 15,000 square miles (about 40,000 sq km) of open areas and 4,000 square miles (about 10,000 sq km) of forest in the state of Roraima.

The Brazilian government lacks the political will to reverse this process of rapacious destruction. In 1999 a ban on new Amazon clearing was revoked at the beginning of the burning season. The government continues to be in thrall to powerful industry and lobbying, while starving its environmental agencies of resources.

Meanwhile, the northeast of Brazil, the most populated semiarid area in the world, with ten million people living in nine states, is suffering its fourteenth drought in 100 years. It is already the worst shortage of rain in the last 15 years and according to the National Institute for Space Research no rain is expected until 2001.

The rain shortfall was compounded, as in the past, by the lack of investment in proven cost-effective, low-technology solutions. Local politicians preferred to lobby for a controversial US $1.5 billion scheme to transport water from the São Francisco River for irrigation.

A look to the future

"If we wished to, we could make of this country a great nation," said Brazil's national hero, Tiradentes. Two hundred years on, Brazil has become an economic power with enormous potential, but remains trapped in an archaic political system of privilege and shocking social inequality. Brazil needs a mental revolution, a reversal of priorities, so that its social development can catch up with its economic development. Otherwise, the currency can change, the president can change, the capital be moved, but Brazil risks remaining, in the third millennium, the land of the future.

WHERE TO GO, WHAT TO SEE

Wherever you go in Brazil, the language is Portuguese and the passion football (soccer), but each region has a very distinctive flavor. The distances are huge, so it makes sense to get an air pass before you go.

Rail Travel

Railroads are rare, run-down, and slow. The exceptions are the breathtakingly beautiful line that runs past waterfalls and across gorges from Curitiba down to the port of Paranaguá on the Paraná coast. Or in the North, the thrice-weekly, sixteen-hour trip which takes you 550 miles southwest from São Luis to the iron ore mine at Carajás in the Eastern Amazon. The nightly train that runs between Rio and São Paulo has been privatized, modernized, and renamed the Silver Train. You can now wine and dine aboard but a sleeping cabin will cost you $100.

Buses

Hitchhiking is not much practiced and anyway buses are plentiful and cheap. Half of Brazil always seems to be traveling: buses and bus terminals are always crowded. Slightly more expensive are the *onibus leito* (literally, bed-buses), which offer you a fully reclining seat and unlimited coffee and mineral water as they roll through the night or day.

Rio de Janeiro

Rio's reputation as one of the most beautiful cities in the world has been tarnished by its more recent fame as a violent, dangerous place to walk around. Behave as you would in any big city – leave your valuables and passport in the hotel, take nothing to the beach, and keep your eyes open.

Ouro Preto

Eight hours from Rio, ten hours from São Paulo, Ouro Preto, recognized by UNESCO as the most complete eighteenth century colonial town in the world, is a tightly-packed mass of cobbled streets, houses, and richly decorated churches, built with the gold of the local mines. Look for Aleijadinho's work, scattered in different places. Semi-precious stones and soapstone artifacts are on sale everywhere.

Salvador

Brazil's capital when the slave trade was at its height, it still has the highest proportion of black people. Syncretism has produced a unique mix of Catholic and African candomblé religions. Musical creativity is at its height

Ouro Preto

Tony Morrison/South American Pictures

in Salvador, with the powerful drumbeat of Olodum and other mass percussion bands echoing round the cobbled streets, the annual invention of new Carnival rhythms blaring out to the massed crowds that dance behind the *trios elétricos* (mobile band platforms) and the gentle twang of the *berimbau* player. South or north of Salvador is lotus-eater's paradise – soft sandy beaches where you can lie under palm trees sipping from a fresh coconut and snacking on freshly-caught seafood. Brazil's Atlantic coastline offers hundreds of beaches, some exploited, many unspoiled.

Belém

Built round an old fort on the mouth of the Amazon, the streets are lined with ancient mango trees. Ver o Peso is an open air waterfront market selling charms, herbs, and essences guaranteed to cure every conceivable physical and emotional problem, from cancer to unfaithfulness.

Marajó

A boat or plane ride takes you from Belém to the world's biggest river island, home to herds of wild and domesticated buffalo. Even the police ride buffalo instead of horses.

The Amazon

To get a feeling of the real width of the mighty Amazon, travel upriver to Santarém, where the Tapajós river flows into it. Buy a hammock and a length of rope and go down to the quayside where the riverboats wait for the evening tide to sail to Oriximina or Obidos. Join the other passengers in the forest of gently swaying hammocks, fall asleep to the throbbing of the engine as the boat chugs across the river, with the moon shining on the water. Wake at dawn and discover you have exchanged the open sea of the Amazon for the confines of a river. A slug of coffee from the communal thermos flask, a quick wash, and you can stand at the rail and watch life on the riverbank, children splashing and swimming, women washing clothes, men silently paddling canoes.

Manaus

A thousand miles upriver from the sea is the Amazon capital, where the few reminders of the rubber boom include the beautiful l00-year-old Opera House, and the floating dock built to accommodate an annual tidal rise and fall of up to 50 feet. Manaus is now reachable by road from the south but the main highway into the depths of the Amazon remains the river, with boats of all sizes carrying cargo and passengers.

Pantanal

One of the world's largest wildlife areas, these vast wetlands lie in the west of Brazil, spilling over into Bolivia and Paraguay. There are over 600 bird species and river banks lined with sunbathing caiman alligators and herds of capivara (the world's largest rodent). You can take boat trips from Corumbá, a sleepy, baking-hot waterfront town on the Paraguai river, while from Campo Grande and Cuiabá, you can join safaris or reach ranch-hotels.

Rio Grande do Sul

Along with Santa Catarina, Brazil's most southern states offer a temperate climate and a strong German and Italian influence, present in food, architecture, and last names. But the characteristic barbecue (*churrasco*) and mate tea (*chimarrão*) are customs inherited from the original inhabitants of the rolling pampas and valleys, the Indians.

TIPS FOR TRAVELLERS

People

Brazilians respond much better to a smile than a shout, to a joke rather than an insult. Don't be afraid of physical contact: Brazilians, like other Latins, do not have the same horror of touching each other that most Anglo-Saxons have. Everyone shakes hands all the time, friends and often mere acquaintances kiss once, twice, or even three times on the cheek, men pat or thump each other on the back. When they are talking to each other Brazilians not only wave their hands around but feel the need to touch the person they are talking to.

Safety

Brazil has a reputation for petty crime, especially in the big cities like Rio, São Paulo, and Recife, where muggers and bag snatchers are common and tourists are fair game. However, you can reduce the risks by taking a few basic precautions.

Be streetwise – leave passports, travelers checks and money in the hotel safe and carry only small amounts of cash when you go out. Take your camera in an ordinary plastic bag, not around your neck. Don't wear expensive jewelry or watches. In Rio and other seaside resorts, take as little as possible to the beach. Even clothes get stolen while you are swimming! Don't walk on Rio's Copacabana beach at night, it's a notorious mugging spot. Don't visit shanty-towns unless accompanied by somebody who knows the residents.

Health

Taking a few precautions can also avert health problems which can spoil your trip, or worse. Don't drink tap water – mineral water is generally available; don't eat unwashed lettuce or fruit – market gardeners use liberal amounts of pesticide; and don't overdo the sunbathing, especially around midday.

You only have to worry about malaria if you are going away from the main tourist centers into certain areas of the Amazon. It is more prevalent during the rainy season, which runs from October to April. Mosquito nets can be purchased at any Amazon town.

If you pick up some form of bug or parasite, go to an English-speaking Brazilian doctor because he will be more familiar with the symptoms.

Pharmacies sell over the counter many medicines and drugs that would be available on prescription only in UK and the U.S.. Tampons and similar items are sold everywhere in pharmacies and supermarkets, as are condoms.

Women Travelers

It is becoming more and more common to see women traveling on their own, eating on their own. Except in the more remote places, lone women should not encounter any problems.

Changing Money

Dollars and travelers checks can now be changed at many banks, travel agencies, and exchange (Cambio) shops. Hotels also exchange money, but give a lower rate. Don't be confused by the existence of three different rates – commercial, tourist and "parallel," the Brazilian euphemism for black market. There is almost no difference between them, so it is best to change at a bank, agency, or shop. Outside the main cities, changing money is much more difficult, and international credit cards are not always acceptable, so it is best to change sufficient before you travel to the interior.

Souvenirs

The best places to buy souvenirs are in the open air markets. Never accept the first price, always haggle.
São Paulo: Praça da Republica and Praça de Liberdade (oriental fair). Markets are held on Saturdays and Sundays.
Rio: Praça General Osorio and along the beaches.
Belém: Ver o Peso market, renowned for charms and potions of all sorts.
The government's Indian affairs agency, FUNAI, runs shops at the major airports which offer indigenous artifacts at reasonable prices.

Children

Because of baby trafficking and pedophile scandals, foreigners taking small children or babies out of Brazil may be required to prove their relationship with them. If traveling with children, be prepared for this by taking their birth certificates with you.

Drugs

Brazilian prisons are crowded with foreigners caught attempting to smuggle out drugs, sometimes just a few grams. Brazil is a major corridor for cocaine produced in Bolivia, Colombia, and Peru: the police are very alert; the sentences are long, and prison conditions are harsh. Don't risk it.

ADDRESSES AND CONTACTS

BRAZIL

Brasília

British Embassy, Setor de Embaixadas Sul, Quadra 801, Conjunto K. Tel: 225 2710

Canadian Embassy, Av. das Nacões, Q803, lote 16, sl. 130 Tel: 321 2171

U.S. Embassy, Av. das Nacões, lote 3. Tel: 321 7272 or 224 9344 (after hours)

Curitiba

British Trade Office, Rua Presidente Faria 51, 7 andar, Tel: 322 1202

Porto Alegre

British Commercial Office Rua Antenor Lemos 57 Conjunto 403 Tel: 249 1060; 249 6688

U.S. Consulate, Rua Cel. Genuino 421. Tel: 226 4177

Recife

British Consulate, Av. Marques de Olinda 200, room 410, 4th floor. Tel: 2214 0650

U.S. Consulate, Rua Gonçalves Maia 163, Boa Vista. Tel: 221 1412/1413, 222 6577/6612

Rio de Janeiro

British Consulate-General Praia do Flamengo, 284/2 andar Tel: 553 3223

Canadian Consulate, Rua Lauro Müller 116, Room 1104, Torre Rio Sul, Botofago. Tel: 275 2137

U.S. Consulate, Av. Presidente Wilson 147, Centro. Tel: 292 7117

São Paulo

British Consulate-General Av. Paulista 37, 17 andar. Tel: 287 7722

Canadian Consulate, Av. Paulista 854, Bela Vista Tel: 285 5099

USA AND CANADA

Amaaka'a Amazon Network, 339 Lafayette St., New York, NY 10003

Global Exchange, 2017 Mission St., Rm. 303, San Francisco, CA 94110. Tel: (415) 255 7296, organizes "Reality Tours" to a number of countries, including Brazil. These provide participants with a chance to meet local people and learn about the most pressing issues facing the country. Also Women-to-Women Exchanges, which sets up internships with Brazilian women's organizations.

News from Brazil, PO Box 42536, Los Angeles, CA 90050-0536, monthly magazine with 60 pages on politics, culture, soccer news, etc.

Rainforest Action Network, 450 Sansome St., Suite 700, San Francisco, CA 94111. Tel: (415) 398 4404.

Rising Youth for Social Equity (RYSE), 2017 Mission St., 3rd floor, San Francisco, CA 94110. Tel: (415) 863 1100. Fax: (415) 863 9798. Email: kidryse@aol.com, builds links between U.S. and Brazilian youth to organize for positive social change.

50 Years Is Enough Coalition, 1025 Vermont Ave, NW, Suite 300, Washington DC 20005. Tel: (202) 879 3197. Works on World Bank and structural adjustment issues.

BRITAIN

Action Brazil, 26A Chatsworth Road, London NW2 4BS, promotes "Campaign Against Hunger in Brazil", raising funds and sending second-hand clothes to Brazil.

Brazil Network, PO Box 1325, London SW9 0RA, links individuals and organizations working on Brazil and interested in keeping up to date on events. Publishes a quarterly newsletter.

Brazilian Arts and Community Centre, 1 Elgin Avenue, London W9, provides a range of services for the Brazilian community.

Brazilian Contemporary Arts, Palingswick House, 241 King St., London W6 9LP, organizes cultural events and publishes a regular newsletter.

Brazilian Embassy, 32 Green St., London W1Y 4AT, the embassy has an Internet site on http://www.demon.co.uk/Itamaraty/, with a range of economic, political and other information on Brazil.

Leros, 25A Collingbourne Rd., London W12 0SG.
Free Portuguese-language magazine for the Brazilian community in Britain.

Workers Party (PT), PO Box 3698, London SW2 1XB. Contact for its London branch. Organizes events, fund-raising.

Task Brasil, 140 Bermondsey St., London SE1 3TX.
New organization, planning to set up a network of shelters for street children in Brazil.

FURTHER READING AND BOOKSTORES

Fiction

Amado J., *Dona Flor and Her Two Husbands*, New York, 1969
Amado J., *The War of the Saints*, New York, 1993
de Andrade M., *Macunaíma*, New York, 1984
Dourado A., *A Hidden Life*, New York, 1969
Lispector C., *Family Ties*, Austin, Texas, 1972
Lispector C., *The Hour of the Star*, Manchester, 1986
Machado de Assis, J.M., *Epitaph of a Small Winner*, New York, 1952
Machado de Assis, J.M., *Dom Casmurro*, New York, 1953
Machado de Assis, J.M., *Philosopher or Dog*, New York, 1954
de Queirós R., *The Three Marias*, Austin, Texas, 1963
Ramos G., *Childhood*, London, 1979
Ribeiro D., *Maíra*, New York, 1984
Ribeiro J.U., *An Invincible Memory*, New York, 1988
Souza M., *The Emperor of the Amazon*, New York, 1977
Torres A., *The Land*, London, 1987

Non Fiction: Politics and Society

Branford, S. and Kucinski, B., *Brazil, Carnival of the Oppressed: Lula and the Brazilian Workers' Party*, London, 1995
Caipora, *Women in Brazil*, London, 1993
de Castro, J., *Death in the Northeast: Poverty and Revolution in the Northeast of Brazil*, New York, 1966
da Cunha, E., *Rebellion in the Backlands*, Chicago, 1957
Dannaher, K. and Shellenberger, M. (eds), *Fighting for the Soul of Brazil*, New York, 1995
Dimenstein, G., *Brazil: War on Children*, London, 1991
Freyre, G., *The Masters and The Slaves*, New York, 1964
Guillermoprieto, A., *Samba*, London, 1990
Keck, M., *The Workers' Party and Democratization in Brazil*, New Haven, 1992
de Jesus, C.M., *Beyond All Pity: The Diary of Carolina Maria de Jesus*, London, 1990
Macauley, N., *Dom Pedro: The Struggle for Liberty In Brazil and Portugal*, Durham NC, 1986
Scheper-Hughes, N., *Death Without Weeping: The Violence of Everyday Life in Brazil*, Berkeley, 1992
Sutton, A., *Slavery in Brazil*, London, 1995

Non Fiction: Amazon and the Environment

Branford, S. and Glock,O., *The Last Frontier: Fighting Over Land in the Amazon*, London, 1985

Cummings, B., *Dam the Rivers, Damn the People: Development and Resistance in Amazonian Brazil*, London, 1990

Hecht, S. and Cockburn, A., *The Fate of the Forest*, London, 1990

Hemming, J., *Red Gold: The Conquest of the Brazilian Indians*, London, 1995

Hemming, J., *Amazon Frontier: The Defeat of the Brazilian Indians*, London, 1995

Macmillan, G., *At the End of the Rainbow? Gold, Land and People in the Brazilian Amazon*, London, 1995

Mendes, C. and Gross, T., *Fight for the Forest: Chico Mendes in his Own Words*, London, 1992

Fr. Ricardo Rezende, *Rio Maria: Song of the Earth*, London, 1994

Bookstores in Brazil

São Paulo

Cultura, Conjunto Nacional, Avenida Paulista 2073, Cerqueira César, has a big selection of English-language books, as do *Bestseller*, Av. Tietê 184, Cerqueira César and *Kosmos*, Av. São Luis 162, Centro. More English-language books, along with a wide selection of Portuguese-language work, can be found at *Brasiliense*, Rua Barão de Ipateninga 99, Seridó.

Recife

Livro 7, Rua Sete de Setembro 329, in the city center, has foreign-language books.

Rio de Janeiro

For English language books, try the various branches of *Unilivros*, scattered all over Rio, e.g. at the Largo do Machado (Flamengo) and at Av. Ataúlfo de Paiva 686 (Leblon).

FACTS AND FIGURES

GEOGRAPHY

Official Name: República Federativa do Brasil
Situation: Between 5° 16" N and 33° 45" South, and between 35° and 74° West. Occupies most of eastern-central part of South America, with 92% of the country located between the Equator and the Tropic of Capricorn. Four different time zones. Maximum north-south distance 2678 m.; east-west 2683 m.
Surface Area: 3,282,226 sq.m., (approx same size as USA, 35 times the size of the United Kingdom). Covers 21% of the Americas and 47% of South America. The Amazon region (Amazonia Legal) covers 1.9 million sq.m., 60% of Brazil's total area.
Frontiers: 9,746 m. of land frontiers with nine other countries: Argentina, Uruguay, Paraguay, Bolivia, Peru, Colombia, Surinam, Guyana, and French Guyane.
Administrative division: Brazil is a federal republic with 26 states and 1 federal district (Brasília).
Capital: Brasília, 1.3 million inhabitants
Other Cities: There are 9 metropolitan areas with over 1 million inhabitants, the largest being São Paulo with 17 million and Rio de Janeiro with 10 million. Belo Horizonte and Salvador have over 2 million, and Salvador, Belém, Fortaleza, Curitiba, and Porto Alegre over 1 million (1991 census).
Infrastructure and travel: 990,000 m. of roads, but only 9% paved (1993). Uruguay, Paraguay, Argentina, Bolivia, Peru, Venezuela, and Guyana can be reached by road. Some excellent expressways in the São Paulo area.
Air travel: excellent network connects Brazil with Europe, North and South America, Africa, and Asia. All major Brazilian cities and many smaller ones reachable by air: three national private airlines (Varig, Vasp, Transbrasil) plus several regional carriers.
Railroads: 13,600 m. of track, divided into six regional networks.
Passenger services Rio-São Paulo, Curitiba-Paranagua (most scenic), São Paulo-Santos, São Paulo-Brasília, São Luis-Carajás.
Commuter networks in Rio, São Paulo, and other large cities very overcrowded, ancient rolling stock, badly maintained.
São Paulo and Rio have very modern, efficient but limited metro systems.
Waterways: the Amazon region has 50,000m. of navigable water-ways: passenger boats and cargo boats taking passengers ply all the main rivers (cabins and hammocks).
Ports: South Atlantic ports: Santos, Rio de Janeiro, Rio Grande, Tubarão, Paranaguá. North Atlantic: Belém and São Luis
Relief and landscape: Brazil's vast areas offers great variety, from the rainforest in the north to the *caatinga* drylands in the Northeast. North of the Amazon the rainforest changes to savannah before reaching the Surinamese and Guyanese borders. The Pantanal wetlands in the west cover 58,000 sq.m., extending into Bolivia and Paraguay, and are home to thousands of species of birds, reptiles and mammals. Between the Amazon region and the caatinga region there is a fertile transition zone of undulating hills covered in palm trees. Central Brazil is a plateau of open plains with twisted trees and acid soils (*cerrados*). In the South little is left of the once extensive pine (araucaria) forests and only 8% remains of the Atlantic Forest which once covered the entire Atlantic seaboard.

Brazil's 4,500 m. of sea-coast include thousands of attractive palm-fringed beaches. Brazil's most mountainous regions are the central state of Minas Gerais and the southern state of Santa Catarina. The highest peak is the 9886ft. Pico da Neblina on the Amazon border with Venezuela.

Temperature and rainfall: in most of Brazil the climate is tropical with temperatures rarely under 65°F. In Rio summer temperatures can reach the 100s. In São Paulo winter (July-August) temperatures can fall to under 50°F. Snow occasionally falls in the southern states of Santa Catarina and Rio Grande do Sul, when below freezing temperatures are recorded. In São Paulo and Rio summer (December-March) rainstorms often lead to extensive flooding.

Fauna: there are no large wild animals in Brazil but many smaller ones and thousands of bird, fish, and insect species. 36 species, including jaguars, monkeys, and anteaters are considered to be in danger of extinction.

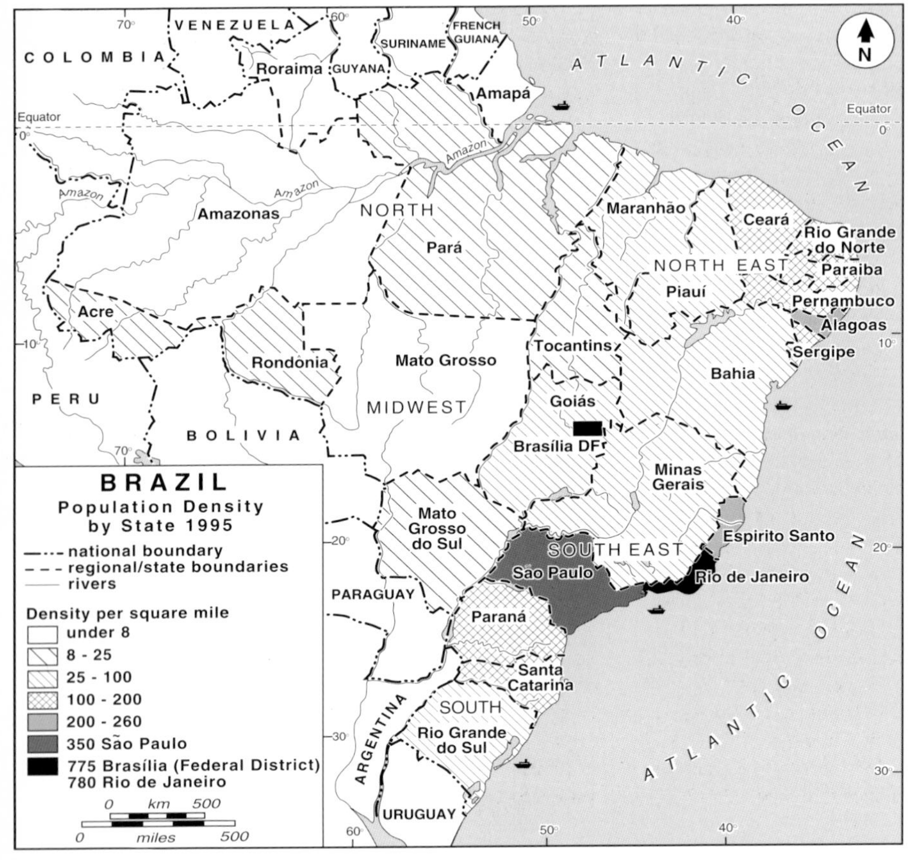

POPULATION

Population (1995): 155.8 million. Sixth largest in world.
Population growth (cumulative): 1980-1991: 23.3% (urban 37.9%, rural -7.0%)
Population density: 45.8 inhabitants per sq.m. (world average 98 per sq.m.)
Urbanization: 75% live in cities and towns, most of them on or near the coast.
Age structure: rapid changes due to the fall in family size: percentage of under 15s will fall from 35% to 24% by the year 2020, while over 65s rise to 8% of population.
Fertility rate: 2.7 children per woman of reproductive age in 1990, compared to 6.1 in 1940
Birth rate: 1.7% (1990-95), 3% (1960-69)
Infant mortality rate (1994): 56/1000; 156/1,000 (1950s)
Average life expectancy (1993): women: 68.9 years, men: 64.1
Adult illiteracy (1993): 17.6% (10% in São Paulo, 40% in Piauí)
Education: primary education is free between 7 and 14 (8 years), secondary education is free 14-18 (4 years). Only 50% of school-age children are in school.
UNDP Human Development Index (1995): 63rd out of 174
Language: Portuguese, and 170 indigenous languages spoken by Brazil's 320,000 Indians.
Ethnic composition (1991 census): Whites 54%, blacks 6%, mestiços (mixed race) 39%. The proportion of whites and blacks if falling, while that of mestiços is rising.
Religion: Roman Catholicism remains the majority religion, but the numbers are falling steadily. An estimated 15% (and rising) belongs to Protestant, including Pentecostal Churches. 3.5 million belong to the fastest growing Pentecostal Church, the Universal Church of the Kingdom of God. The national statistical institute (IBGE) estimates that up to 1.5% of heads of families follows Afro-Brazilian religions such as candomblé and umbanda, while the Afro-Brazilian Federation says 70 million Brazilians have links with them.
Sources: Instituto Brasileiro de Geografia e Estadística (IBGE); UNDP; World Bank, Europa Yearbook of South America, Central America and the Caribbean

HISTORY AND POLITICS

Some key dates.
1500 Pedro Alvares Cabral sights land and names it "Land of the True Cross"* 1530 first African slaves arrive in Brazil * 1630-1695 Palmares Quilombo* 1789 Conspiracy discovered to overthrow Portuguese rule and declare republic * 1792 Tiradentes, one of plotters, hung, drawn, and quartered * 1808 Portuguese court moves to Brazil * 1822 Independence of Brazil declared. Pedro I becomes emperor * 1865 Brazil, Argentina, and Uruguay form Triple Alliance and declare war on Paraguay * 1888 Slavery abolished * 1889 Republic declared * 1924 Prestes column begins march * 1930 Getúlio Vargas leads a revolution, President Washington Luis deposed * 1932 São Paulo oligarchy declares constitutional revolution against Vargas * 1937 Getúlio Vargas creates Estado Nôvo, a populist dictatorship * 1942 Brazil enters Second World War in support of the Allies * 1954 Vargas commits suicide * 1960 Brasília, Brazil's new capital, inaugurated * 1961 President Jânio Quadros resigns, setting off political crisis that leads to military coup three years later *

1964 Military overthrow President João Goulart * 1968 President Costa e Silva closes Congress and introduces repression with Decree AI-5 * 1979 Amnesty introduced by military * 1985 Tancredo Neves, first civilian president after 21 year military regime, dies before taking office. Vice-president José Sarney becomes president * 1986 President Sarney introduces Cruzado Plan, the first of series of unsuccessful economic plans designed to tame inflation * 1987 Brazil declares moratorium on foreign debt repayments * 1989 First direct presidential elections since 1960. Fernando Collor elected after using dirty tricks to defeat left-wing trade unionist Luis Inácio Lula da Silva * 1992 President Collor resigns to avoid impeachment * 1994 President Itamar Franco introduces Real Plan to curb inflation * 1994 Fernando Henrique Cardoso elected President

Constitution: presidential republic: election for 5-year term by universal suffrage (over 16 years). Legislative power is exercised by the 81-seat senate and the 513-seat chamber of deputies, elected for 4- year terms by universal suffrage. The size of legislative assemblies in each state varies according to its population.

Head of state: Fernando Henrique Cardoso (term began Jan. 1995)

Congress: main parties (numbers fluctuate) are Partido da Social-Democracia Brasileira (PSDB, Party of Brazilian Social Democracy); the right-wing Partido da Frente Liberal (PFL, Party of the Liberal Front; the centrist Partido do Movimento Democrático Brasileiro (PMDB, Party of the Brazilian Democratic Movement); the right-wing Partido Progressista Brasileiro, (PPB, Brazilian Progressive Party), former pro-military Arena); the left-wing Partido dos Trabalhadores (PT, Workers Party), and the center-left Partido Democrático Trabalhista (PDT, Democratic Labor).

Armed Forces: Total armed forces in 1994 comprised 336,800. Of these, 219,000 were in the army (including 126,500 conscripts); 58,400 in the navy (2,000 conscripts) and 59,400 in the air force (5,000 conscripts).

Membership of international organizations: UN and UN agencies, Organization of American States, Rio Group (with other South American states, plus Mexico), Mercosul (with Argentina, Uruguay, and Paraguay), G77, Latin American Integration Association, International Monetary Fund

Media/communications: There are 15.5 million telephones, including 1.6 million mobiles (1995). Daily newspapers with national distribution are *Folha de S.Paulo*, *O Globo*, *O Estado de São Paulo*, *Jornal do Brasil*, and *Gazeta Mercantil.* The main weekly news magazines are *Veja*, and *Isto É.* There are 257 TV Stations. The largest commercial networks are Globo, Manchete, SBT, Bandeirantes. TV Cultura (São Paulo state) and TVE (Rio de Janeiro state), as well as satellite and cable systems. There are 2765 AM and FM radio stations (1991).

ECONOMY

Currency: real (R$); R$ = $ June 1994: 0.78, June 96: 1.01

Inflation: 1993: 2,708.55%, 1994: 1,312.43%, 1995: 12.97%* (Fundaçao Getúlio Vargas)

Gross domestic product (GDP): $688 billion (1995), ninth largest in the world (World Bank)

Economic growth: 1995: 4.2%; 1994: 5.8%; 1993: 4.2%; 1992: -0.9%; 1991: 0.3%; 1990: -4.4%